BOMBS
AWAY

Fifty Old, Often Bad, and Mostly Forgotten Films, in No Particular Order

JOHN VETTO

Published by Wheatmark®
2030 East Speedway Boulevard, Suite 106
Tucson, Arizona 85719 USA
www.wheatmark.com

ISBN: 979-8-88747-114-3 (paperback)
ISBN: 979-8-88747-115-0 (ebook)
LCCN: 2023912787

Bulk ordering discounts are available through Wheatmark, Inc. For more information, email orders@wheatmark.com or call 1-888-934-0888.

rev202301
rev202402
rev202403

To Irene and Marcia,
I finally did it!

Contents

Acknowledgments

I should reveal that I am a surgeon, so I begin this book with a quote from a fellow surgeon:

> *No one accomplishes anything in this life on his or her own. Even when we stare in awe at what might appear to be a solitary feat . . . there is invisible support. There are loved ones at home who cherish the adventure. A mentor to teach. A colleague with whom the experience can be shared. And unseen magic too.*
>
> —Allan J. Hamilton, The Scalpel and the Soul

Well, I don't think anyone will be staring at this book with awe or noting any magic, but it was definitely not a solitary feat. No, I have many others with whom I need to share the credit— or the blame. In chronological order:

1. My dad and my brothers, who turned me on to "bombs"
2. My wife, Irene, who encouraged me and allowed me the time away from my already limited moments with her and family to write this thing
3. My friends and colleagues, especially fellow author Nawzad Othman, who encouraged me to publish it, and

John Mozena, who actually read the whole thing and appeared to enjoy it

4. Mark DePaul, my Publishing Consultant, Lori Conser, my Editor, and their staff at Wheatmark, who made it happen

And, of course, all the people who created these films. Well, not really. Like me, they just wanted to get a little recognition and maybe make a buck. With one exception—Donald C. Rogers, whose work, stories, and gracious permission made Chapter 45 possible.

And here comes my whiny disclaimer: The opinions expressed in this book are those of the author, and they are just that—opinions. The stories related in the book are commonly known in movie lore and have been gleaned from the most reliable sources the author could find—which, given the topic, is not saying much. The author takes no responsibility for the absolute accuracy of all the "facts" he discovered pulling this material together. So there.

Preface

Believe it or not, this book started out about nine years ago as a novel. It was a story about a Medical Oncologist with an anger problem who gets into a car accident with a reformed alcoholic who teaches him how to conquer his anger and control issues. Not only was it pretty bad, but I realized that I was ripping off the plot of *Changing Lanes* (2002). So, I decided to change it to a nonfiction book describing my experiences as a Surgical Oncologist and my deep belief in the importance of personal contact in cancer care—sitting close to people, looking at their faces, touching them. I was about halfway through when COVID-19 hit. Needless to say, the book went on hold.

All of these experiences forced me to reevaluate why I was writing, and I realized that after writing over 188 scientific papers, I wanted to try something else. You see, science and medical writing follow rigid rules—I am also a journal editor and know them well—leaving little opportunity for free expression, loose grammar, or fun with writing. Don't get me wrong—I'm proud of my footprint in PubMed—but I realized that by writing something for lay audiences, I was looking to break free of those set writing conventions I use every day. I wanted to write sentences that began with a preposition or were incomplete. Like this. Or this.

And so, I went back to the drawing board and followed the old adage "Write about what you know." I know something about two things: medicine and old movies. Having tried to write about medicine twice, I decided to give old movies a try.

I love films, especially old and not particularly great films. I love to notice things in these movies and draw connections to other films and to cinema and real-life history. My love of these movies began when I was a kid. On the weekends, my dad and brothers would sit down at night and watch bad movies on the late-late shows such as *Science Fiction Theater* and *Night Cap Theater with Stu Martin*, shows that showcased old action and sci-fi movies on KPTV, Channel 12, the local independent station, or KOIN, Channel 6, the CBS affiliate, in our hometown of Portland, Oregon.

My dad called these movies *bombs*, as in "Hey, guys, let's watch a bomb!" I don't know if he made this term up or heard it somewhere, but we all understood it was a term of affection. My dad was a highly successful medical professional, but he loved things like watching bombs and rooting for underdogs. He knew that in the end, the movie would be a dud, and the underdog would lose, but it was still fun to watch these films. Years before *Mystery Science Theater 3000* relentlessly made fun of these films, we actually watched them for their entertainment value, which included the fact that they were bad, cheap, or already forgotten.

I was somewhat horrified a few years later to discover that film critic Leonard Maltin also used the term *bomb* to describe films but reserved it for the worst of the worst. I wouldn't define bombs that way. My definition of *bomb* is broad and includes a lot of films that vary in terms of age, quality, and genre. Supreme Court justice Potter Stewart once said about obscenity/pornography that he couldn't define it, "but I know it when

I see it." Similarly, I can't always define a bomb, but I know one when I see it. Also, a bomb is not necessarily a cult film. Many films receive cult status for various reasons. To me, a bomb may be forgotten, undiscovered, dated, silly, whatever—but I know a bomb when I see one because it's *fun* to watch.

A point of clarity: labeling a film a *bomb* does not mean it bombed at the box office (i.e., lost money). A lot of very good films lost money when they first came out. Disney's 2009 *A Christmas Carol* is a great version of the classic story that I watch every year, yet it lost almost $100 million initially. *Citizen Kane* (1941) lost money during its initial run, largely due to political reasons. *The Wizard of Oz* (1939) lost MGM over a million dollars—an almost unbelievable loss at the time—at its initial run but made up big-time in rerelease. Less surprisingly, a lot of really bad films, what Maltin would call *bombs*, also bombed at the box office. The best example is the simply terrible *Heaven's Gate* (1980), which made only $4.5 million against its $44 million cost. In contrast, some films that I consider bombs actually made a few dollars for their creators because the films were often made for so little money.

Disclaimer 1: I do not rate films I review here; I leave that to professionals. To me, all movies are interesting in some way. Despite the title of this tome, the order of the fifty films included here actually does follow a bit of logic—but if you can follow it, that suggests you can glimpse into my brain, and I take no responsibility for that.

Disclaimer 2: I am not woke. The films I review here were definitely not woke. Ergo ipso facto, this book is not woke. In fact, after nine years of surgical training and subsequent years of being on call, I am so chronically sleep-deprived that I basically wrote this book in my sleep. Therefore, if you are Easily Offended, please do not read it. More so, if you are the kind of person who looks into things to become Easily Offended, definitely do not read it. Trust me, you'll be Easily Offended. These films are fragments of history, and, like Popeye, they are what they are. You can take up your complaints with the people who made them. Wait, most of them are dead. Never mind.

He Walked by Night (1948) and Its
Connection to a Certain Detective Series

Sixteen years before he appeared as Admiral Nelson in *Voyage to the Bottom of the Sea* (1964–1968), a young Richard Basehart played the psychopathic cop killer in this little film noir gem, made in pseudo-documentary style by the great cinematographer John Alton and codirected by an uncredited Anthony Mann. This was one of many B pictures Basehart did, often playing the villain—as in *The House on Telegraph Hill* (1951)—before finding some success in bigger films like *Moby Dick* (1956) and *The Brothers Karamazov* (1958). Like other action B pictures, *He Walked by Night* moves quickly through its seventy-eight-minute running time to a sudden conclusion, in this case an exciting shootout in the storm drains of LA, a set piece that predated the ending of *The Third Man* (1949) by a year.

If this were all there was to *He Walked by Night*, it would be an entertaining but forgettable piece of American film history. But from the film's beginning, the viewer notices something about the movie that instantly brings to mind a certain radio and

TV detective series. The opening credits list an actor named Jack Webb at the bottom of the starring list, and then the film begins with the words "This story is true . . . only the names have been changed to protect the innocent." This is followed by a narrated series of stock scenes of LA, telling the viewer about that city before dissolving into the crime story. And so the viewer looks for Mr. Webb, and there he is, surprisingly, in an unassuming role as a somewhat mousy crime lab technician who is kidded about not being a "real detective" yet provides valuable clues early on. He then helps orchestrate the construction of a suspect sketch from an assembly of robbery victims that looks exactly like...Richard Basehart! Webb's role emphasized the importance of the crime lab technician, a point often stressed in episodes of *Dragnet*—of course, that's the program I'm alluding to—by a character usually named Lee Jones and frequently played by Olan Soule.

Indeed, it was during the filming of *He Walked by Night* in 1948 that Webb struck up a friendship with the film's technical adviser, Detective Sergeant Marty Wynn, and came up with the idea for *Dragnet*. By the time Webb's new show appeared on radio one year later, and then on TV starting in 1951 and as a revival in 1967, Webb had graduated to a "real detective" named Joe Friday, exuding a toughness that the actor had developed in such radio shows as the edgy *Pat Novack for Hire* (1946–1947) and *Jeff Regan, Investigator* (1948). *Dragnet* went on to become arguably the most influential detective series in entertainment history, and it all started with this little B film.

Having dropped a few names above, I want to point out something that the astute bomb lover has probably already noticed: *He Walked by Night* has a detective named Marty, one named Jones, and Webb's character is named Lee. Webb was a productive and creative person, but, apparently, he didn't think too hard about character names.

And here is a question at the beginning of this book to test your cinephile level: watch this film—it's in the public domain, so you can see it for free; more about that later—but *skip* the opening credits. Then look for a character named Paul Reeves, an electronics salesman who has some unfortunate experiences with Basehart's evil character, Roy. Quick: who plays Paul? Answer below.

A sidenote: another piece of *Dragnet* foreshadowing is actually the Jimmy Stewart western *Bend in the River* (1952), a film, coincidentally, also directed by Anthony Mann. That movie paired Webb with his future *Dragnet* revival costar, Henry (Harry) Morgan. Interestingly, Webb and Morgan play bad guys who come to a bad end, which is kind of fun to see.

Back to the question. Answer: Whit Bissell. Bissell, a genuine WASP (he could trace his family back to a Revolutionary War hero) whose first name was short for Whitmer, was one of those ubiquitous character actors you see everywhere; he appeared in over 120 films and TV programs. Bissell was never a lead character, and his work was often uncredited, but his reputation for the three "A's" of customer loyalty—availability, affability, and ability, in that order—led to him appearing in a lot of very good films: *The Red Badge of Courage* (1951), *The Caine Mutiny* (1954), *The Defiant Ones* (1958), *The Manchurian Candidate*—one of my all-time favorite films—(1962), and the now-forgotten but very timely *Seven Days in May* (1964). TV sci-fi nerds like myself recognize Bissell as Lt. General Heywood Kirk in *The Time Tunnel* (1966–1967). That series, by the way, involved a secret government project named Tic-Toc, which has nothing to do with the present-day, and very much *not* a secret, TikTok.

If you could name Bissell, you might not need to read on. But then again, you might be the only kind of person who would want to read on. I hope not. I think the bombness of these films is something younger generations, especially millennials and centennials, should discover so they have a better understanding of where we have been and where we should be going.

Oops . . . preaching over and back to Bissell. He appeared, uncredited, in the wonderful *Invasion of the Body Snatchers* (1956), a film that ends—first spoiler alert but many more to come—with protagonist Kevin McCarthy looking directly at the audience and issuing a warning. It is the beginning of this book, and I now do the same: there are forty-nine more reviews to come, and *He Walked by Night* is one of the better movies I review.

Well, you were warned.

Seven Things I Liked about *Home to Danger* (1951)

1. It's only sixty-four minutes long. You can watch it on a short flight!
2. It's in the public domain. You can watch it for free on YouTube.
3. It's directed by Terrence Fisher, the guy who directed Christopher Lee in a ton of schmaltzy Hammer films. Here is Mr. Fisher before all that, but you can see inklings of his future work in the nutty plot twists, which the cast follows dutifully without missing a beat: Estranged daughter comes home to hear the reading of her father's will. He has cut her out without a penny. No surprise. But wait . . . there's a codicil that leaves her everything! Now some shady character sets out to kill her at a hunting party on her father's estate. But wait . . . the shady character gets shot instead! No one seems to know who the shady character is or why he wanted to get rid of the daughter. But wait . . . the answer may lie in her father's safe, which she can't open! But wait . . . her boyfriend has a friend who's a safecracker. He opens the safe, and it con-

tains narcotics! The daughter and boyfriend are puzzled. They know nothing about narcotics. But wait . . . the safecracker does, and he has a friend! And so on.

4. It opens with a great scene of a British Overseas Air Corporation—later, British Airlines—prop plane landing in London. It's a Boeing Stratocrusier, a huge double-decker passenger plane that Boeing modeled after the B-29 Superfortress, the only propeller planes that carried atomic bombs. The lower deck of the Stratocruiser was a lounge that could serve seventeen passengers at a time, and the upper deck seated one hundred passengers, including sleeping berths. How I would have loved to have experienced the service on one of those flights. I would have even risked the dicey safety record.

5. The film features a pre–*Hell Drivers* (1957), *Guns of Navarone* (1961), and *Zulu* (1964) Stanley Baker, sporting crazy dark hair and playing the dimwitted groundskeeper. He makes spooky, weird claims to the daughter all through the film, but—spoiler alert—wait . . . they all turn out to be true!

6. The daughter is played by Rona Anderson, who played Alice in *Scrooge* (1951), everyone's favorite version of *A Christmas Carol*, which featured the great Alastair Sim as the old miser. As Alice, Ms. Anderson has a total of three scenes in *Scrooge* and does the old movie trick of faking crying by burying her head in her arms. In *Home to Danger*, you get to see Ms. Anderson in just about every scene, dressed in modern clothes—well, modern for 1951, the year both films were made—and looking fairly attractive. Even her teeth look good, which was unusual for a Brit in the '50s. Maybe they were capped.

7. The boyfriend is played by Guy Rolfe, a British wannabe-

leading man who was doing OK career-wise until he tried out for the lead role in *Trio* (1950), a film about a soldier who contracts TB. Prior to filming, Mr. Rolfe actually did contract TB, was replaced by Michel Rennie, and had to take a break from acting; this was before the development of the revolutionary TB drugs INH and Rifampin. The period off of work cost Rolfe his star status, but he returned to B films and TV and actually had a long career. I spent much of the sixty-four-minute running time of *Home to Danger* wondering where I'd seen him before. Then it hit me: he had the title role in William Castle's— see my reviews of *The Fat Man* and *House on Haunted Hill—Mr. Sardonicus* (1961).

Oops . . . the hour's up, and *Home to Danger* is over. The short running time of such B pictures, or *supporting features* as the Brits called them, left a lot of loose ends and much unexplained stuff, and this film is no exception. But wait . . . that cool-looking Stratocruiser alone makes viewing the film worthwhile.

3

Chicago Syndicate (1955): Bomb or Not?

I don't know what to make of *Chicago Syndicate*. On the one hand, it doesn't seem like a bomb; released by Columbia Pictures at a running time of eighty-four minutes—longer than the usual bomb and right at the edge of my attention span—it features good production values, OK noir photography, great stock footage of Chicago in the '50s, and maybe some location shooting, or is it LA doubling for Chicago? On the other hand, it's clearly a B picture: it was directed by B-picture king Fred Sears, who also directed the great *Earth vs. the Flying Saucers* (1956); features no real stars, only character actors; and was obviously made on a budget. The bad guy, who is supposed to be the boss of a big national syndicate, has exactly three employees. The film even reuses furniture from one scene to another, something I haven't seen since the last time I watched *Plan 9 from Outer Space* (1959); a hutch—look it up, people—in the hero's apartment later shows up in the bad guy's office.

The film opens with some *Dragnet*-style narration about crime in Chicago and how it has gone from bootlegging to white-collar syndicates. Then it shows the murder of an accountant named Nelson Kern, shot dead on the street by two of the bad guy's three employees. Enter heavily decorated war accountant—yes, you read that right—Barry Amsterdam, who is recruited by the FBI to infiltrate the bad guy's syndicate to get the financial goods on him and prove he had Kern killed. Amsterdam is played by Dennis O'Keefe, who hit his zenith in fairly good noir films like *Raw Deal*, directed by Anthony Mann. Of most interest to me as a Surgical Oncologist is the fact that O'Keefe, a heavy cigarette smoker—who wasn't then?— died of lung cancer at St. John's Hospital in Santa Monica. That happened thirty years before it housed the John Wayne Cancer Center, which was initially funded by John Wayne after *he* was operated on for lung cancer.

Amsterdam works his way into the bad guy's "empire" of three employees by a series of phony events staged by the FBI and Joyce Kerns, the dead accountant's daughter, who wants to exact revenge for her father's killing. Joyce is played by Allison Hayes, who played the title character in the wonderfully terrible *Attack of the 50-Foot Woman* (1958) and whose career was marred by chronic illness caused by plumbism (lead poisoning).

The smarmy-looking bad guy, Arnold Valent, is played by Paul Stewart, a ubiquitous character actor who played smarmy-looking characters, most notably the cynical butler in *Citizen Kane* (1941). For someone who is supposed to be street smart, Valent is pretty stupid, falling for all of Amsterdam's tricks, until Amsterdam rises to top man in Valent's organization. Come to think of it, that wasn't so hard since—as I mentioned—there were only three employees to begin with, and they were all idiots. Valent comes to trust Amsterdam so much that he takes him on a tour of the "old neighborhood," complete with a viewing of Death Corner, an alleyway where Valent saw gangsters shot and killed when he was a kid—can you say *fore-shadowing*?—and a visit to his sainted mother.

The most interesting character in the movie is Connie, Valent's girlfriend, played by Abbe Lane. Ms. Lane, a real-life torch singer who performed with Xavier Cugat's band, stretches her acting wings here by playing a torch singer who performs in Xavier Cugat's band. Yes, Cugat is in the movie too, renamed Benny Chico and having a dual role as band leader and Connie's handler. He's a better band leader than handler; Connie is always getting drunk, having fits of jealousy, catfighting with Joyce, and threatening to expose Valent's shady deals. Valent responds by having her beaten up by the three goons, which touches off a crazy ending—spoiler alert—involving a chase through underground elevator tubes that connect department stores. I thought that was cool. During the chase, one of goons gets accidentally electrocuted, and our hero stumbles along after getting shot in the leg. He actually takes his belt off and uses it for a tourniquet, and I thought it was miraculous that his baggy pants—they wore them that way in the '50s—didn't fall down. Valent—super-spoiler alert—ends up getting shot in front of Death Corner and dying in the arms of his sainted mother.

OK, I guess it is a bomb. But I'll say this for *Chicago Syndicate*: it's the most exciting movie about war accountants I have seen this year.

Julius Caesar against the Pirates (1962): Viewing One Bomb Leads to Another

Let me be clear: even though I am half Italian, I am not a fan of Sword-and-Sandal films. I generally find them boring, and dubbed soundtracks are not my thing. Unlike Quentin Tarantino, I do not go searching for bad Sword-and-Sandal, Spaghetti Western, Blaxploitation, or Eurotrash films. Looking for bombs among these genres is like shooting fish in a barrel with a machine gun. No, I like to hunt for bombs in subtler places.

However, I sat down and watched *Julius Caesar against the Pirates* out of sheer curiosity; I wanted to see if Abbe Lane could play someone other than a torch singer in Xavier Cugat's band. As mentioned in my review of *Chicago Syndicate*, Ms. Lane was exactly that. In fact, she was married to Mr. Cugat from 1952 to 1964, wedding him when she was only sixteen. She later wrote a book about the tribulations of being married to an older man. Thirty-two years Lane's senior, Cugat was married five times. Lane, who was Mrs. Cugat #4, was known for her sultry singing style and sexy costumes; she was once delayed from appearing on the *Jackie Gleason Show* until she changed her outfit, which was deemed too revealing for television. She was billed as "Too Sexy for Italy," although she had a thirteen-film career there, and when I read the title of this movie, I just had to take a look. I was especially intrigued when I saw that the film poster portrayed Caesar as—wait for it—an action hero!

That action begins in Rome, of course, where the evil emperor Sulla is out to murder all the senators who oppose him, especially Julius Caesar. Caesar is warned by his manservant, who also serves as comic relief throughout the film, that he is going to be arrested. Somewhat to my surprise, our hero leaves his beautiful wife, Cornelia, behind and flees with the manservant and his sidekick "to the sea," which is only a short distance away, despite the fact that Rome is landlocked. They make off on a big fancy raft complete with a tiller that the manservant and sidekick build in no time.

They are picked up by King Nicomedes's navy and taken to his palace. Nicomedes and Caesar are friends, and there is much lying on pillows, eating of grapes, and dancing girl entertainment. One of the slave girls there is Plauzia, played by Ms. Lane, who catches Caesar's goo-goo eyes because she is taller, has a brighter dress, and displays more cleavage than the other women. Nicomedes wants Caesar to stay, but Caesar tells him that he must return to Cornelia, whom he left holding the bag back in Rome.

The next day, Nicomedes puts Caesar and his two pals on a boat back to Rome and also gives him Plauzia as a gift. That seems like a nice gesture, but Nicomedes has an evil ulterior motive: he knows that Plauzia is the fiancé of Hamar the pirate, who has been robbing Nicomedes's ships. With Plauzia as bait, Nicomedes hopes that Hamar will plunder the ship and bring the fury of Rome down on him because Caesar is on board. Hamar and his men do indeed attack the ship; there is much bloodless swordplay and many judo throws. Caesar fights valiantly, but the ship is captured, and Caesar and his friends are held captive by Hamar on his island fortress, where there are more dancing girl shows.

Hamar is played by Gordon Mitchell, a very interesting guy in real life. A veteran of the Battle of the Bulge and many conflicts in the Korean War, Mitchell was a bodybuilder who played some bit roles in big American films like *The Ten Commandments* (1956) before going to Italy to capitalize on the success of Steve Reeves; see my review of *Jailbait*. He ended up starring in over two hundred B pictures, in which his acting is weird and just terrible. Here, for example, Mitchell portrays Hamar by beating his bare chest and bellowing all his lines. Maybe it's just the dubbing, but his character actually says things like "batten down the hatches!" and "son of a jackal!" Hamar is not much of a romantic; he spends his time with fiancé Plauzia screaming jealous statements, pawing her in attempts to show affection, and beating her. Not surprisingly, Plauzia decides she's really not that fond of him.

No, she falls for Caesar because he's a nice guy and so much more cultured. That drives Hamar nuts, and he wants to kill Caesar and his friends. By this time, Nicomedes's plan has backfired; Sulla doesn't care a whip about Caesar and refuses to send his navy after Hamar, even though his admiral begs Sulla to send at least one boat after the pirates. Seems the admiral's daughter, a university student, was on Caesar's boat and is therefore also now Hamar's prisoner.

After Caesar attempts to buy freedom for himself and his now three comrades—sidekick, comic-relief manservant, and university student; still with me?—he manages to escape; join forces with the admiral's fleet, which is coming to the rescue because Sulla up and died; and lead an attack on Hamar's hideout. It all ends with more bloodless swordplay and judo throws, after which the Roman navy—spoiler alert but no big surprise—defeats the pirates. At one point in the skirmish, Plauzia frees our heroes, making Hamar so mad that he chains her up in front of some weird torture gizmo made of a wall of swords that comes closer and closer. Caesar rushes to save her, but, alas, she dies in his arms because the plot demands it; he's a chaste guy, and his wife, Cornelia, is still waiting at home. Caesar gives Plauzia a kiss as she dies. She's gone, but the memory of her mammaries will stay with him; I stole that joke from Pauline Kael. Caesar is pissed, of course, and has a big fight with Hamar, throwing him into the wall of swords. In the final scene, the admiral tells a triumphant Caesar that "all of Rome is waiting" for him, and the music swells.

Yeah, pretty bad. I have a minor in World History, and I remember that in actuality, a twenty-five-year-old Caesar *was* captured by Cilician pirates while sailing the Aegean Sea. He sent off a bunch of men to collect silver to buy his freedom while staying with the pirates for thirty-eight days. During that time, he actually began to boss them around and forced them to listen to his speeches and poetry he had written. They certainly earned their money. He was indeed avoiding Sulla and waiting for him to die and did end up staying with his friend King Nicomedes. In fact, Caesar stayed with Nicomedes so long that rumors began to circulate back in Rome about their relationship. Not surprisingly, these details were replaced by the screenwriters of this film with swordfights and dancing girls.

I did learn one thing from *Julius Caesar against the Pirates*: the word *versus* apparently does not translate into Italian.

Shock (1946): Vincent Price's Career Gets Loaded into the Bomb Bay

Everyone loves Vincent Price, and Hollywood appeared to have loved him too. He earned not one but two stars on the Hollywood Walk of Fame—one for film and one for television—but for my money, he could have earned a third for radio. If you have never heard him as Simon Templar in *The Saint* radio series (1945–1951), you are in for a treat. The shows can be downloaded from radiospirits.com and heard on Radio Classics, SIRIUS channel 148.

Price's career started out so well. Films like *Song of Bernadette* (1943) and *Keys of the Kingdom* (1944) were among his early appearances, and no one but Price could have portrayed the fragile gigolo Shelby Carpenter so wonderfully in Otto Preminger's *Laura* (1944).

But let's face it: as Price's career went along, he was in an increasing number of bombs. His fans glossed it over by saying he was becoming a "master of horror," but from the Roger Corman cheapies, to *two* William Castle films (see my review of *House on Haunted Hill*), to the Dr. Phibes movies—my oldest brother loves them, but I found them *truly* abominable—to the Dr. Goldfoot entries, there seemed to be no paycheck Price would turn down and no bomb he wouldn't appear in. And as one bad movie piled upon another, Price basically began to play the same character over and over, just in different settings: a sad, doomed guy who wanders sad-faced through the running length of the film to that doom. Well, after a careful study of the man's career, I believe his descent into bombhood started here, with this little potboiler released—"Or did it escape?" as that same brother used to ask—in 1946.

Shock begins with a war bride checking into a San Francisco hotel to meet up with her husband, Lt. Paul Stewart, who has just been released from a prisoner of war camp. He is a day late, so his wife, played by Anabel Shaw, who also did bits in *The Horn Blows at Midnight* (1945) and *Gun Crazy* (1950), gets a night to herself. Instead of raiding the mini bar or sending out for pizza, she actually takes Stewart's framed photo out of her suitcase and spends the night pining at it and sleeping fitfully, dreaming that he's outside the room but she can't get to the door. These scenes actually make her look a bit mentally unbalanced, which I guess is the point.

Anyway, she wakes up because she hears a noise outside. She goes to the balcony in time to see a man in an adjacent room murdering his wife by hitting her with a candlestick. Nowadays, people who see such things would simply pull out their cell phones, film it, and post the video on X, but this is 1946, and she is a frail female thing, so she goes into catatonic shock. The next morning, her husband arrives and finds her that way. By the way, Mrs. Stewart stays in shock most of the movie, yet her hair and makeup remain perfect. Lt. Stewart calls the house doctor, who has no experience with catatonic shock but tells Stewart that fortunately there is a very famous expert on the condition, Dr. Cross, who lives—as people did then—in that very hotel. What luck! He is called, and in enters Vincent Price, the very man Mrs. Stewart saw murder his wife. Yes, it was Dr. Cross in the hotel room with the candlestick.

Anyway, Dr. Cross happens to run one of those big Hollywood sanitariums "outside of town" that looks like Tara and is filled with catatonics and assorted schizophrenics. He convinces Lt. Stewart to let him admit his wife there for "treatment" (i.e., sedation). Dr. Cross is really trying to figure out what to do with her because he knows she saw him kill his wife. Meanwhile, he stuffs his wife's body in a big trunk and ships it to his cabin at a mountain lodge. At the sanitarium, Dr. Cross's attempts to keep Mrs. Stewart sedated and quiet are aided by his head nurse, the woman he is having an affair with and the reason he killed his wife. The nurse is played by Lynn Bari, a 20th Century Fox contract player who appeared in over 150 such B pictures, usually playing an evil femme fatale. She is actually best known as the second most popular pinup girl in *Yank Magazine* during World War II, right behind Betty Grable.

At first it seems that Dr. Cross will get away with it. He keeps Mrs. Stewart sedated until she eventually wakes up and recognizes him, but then he successfully convinces her, her husband, and an expert her husband has called in, Dr. Harvey, that Mrs. Stewart is suffering from a common delusion where patients think the sanitorium staff is evil and trying to kill them. That allows Dr. Cross to keep her in the place for more "treatment" (i.e., sedation). Dr. Cross is also able to slip away to the hunting lodge and throw his wife's body down a crevasse, making it look like her death was an accident.

But this is 1946, and the Hays Office was not going to let Dr. Cross and his concubine go unpunished, so things unravel.

The local district attorney suspects Mrs. Cross was murdered, and Dr. Harvey and Lt .Stewart have their suspicions about Dr. Cross. Just as Dr. Cross and his nurse are trying to kill Mrs. Stewart with insulin—spoiler alert—everyone bursts in, and it does not end well for the evil couple. The audience then sees a sad-faced Vincent Price go to his doom, something he then proceeded to do in most of his remaining eighty-five films.

As an aside, *Shock* was directed by Alan L. Werker, who directed 150 B pictures, most of them unremarkable with two notable exceptions: *He Walked by Night*, which he codirected with Anthony Mann—see my previous review—and *The Adventures of Sherlock Holmes* (1939), in my opinion the best of the Basil Rathbone / Nigel Bruce series.

Shock left me with a profound case of monetary sadness; here is a guy who is obviously well off and owns a suite in a hotel, a cabin in a mountain lodge, and a huge sanitarium complete with a big house in the back, yet throws it all away by killing his wife. He could have just divorced her and given her the mountain lodge. I don't think the nurse was much of a skier.

6

Ann Savage: A *Detour* (1945) through Obscurity

In a previous review, I alluded to films in the public domain. While many foreign films and all movies made by the US government are automatically in the public domain, US commercial films are usually only released into the public domain (i.e., can be viewed free, often full length, on YouTube) when their copyrights expire. All film copyrights expire at ninety-five years. Thus, as of 2023, all films made in 1928 or before (i.e., all silent films and *The Jazz Singer*, which came out in 1927) have been in the public domain. Other film copyrights might expire sooner because they were faulty, got hung up in legal battles, or were released by the filmmaker. A lot of film copyrights expire because the filmmaker simply cannot afford to maintain them. Thus, many films in the public domain are B pictures and, well, bombs.

That said, there is a surprising list of non-bombs in the public domain for the reasons I gave above. These include classics and Academy Award winners such as *The Emperor Jones* (1933), *Of Human Bondage* (1934), *My Man Godfrey* (1936), *A Star Is Born* (1937), *His Girl Friday* (1940), *Our Town* (1940), *Meet*

21

John Doe (1941), *Captain Kidd* (1945), *The Snows of Kilimanjaro* (1952), *The Strange Loves of Martha Ivers* (1946), *The Man with the Golden Arm* (1955), *Charade* (1963), and even, yes, *It's a Wonderful Life* (1946). The list also includes lesser-known thrillers that I love, such as *The Stranger* (1946), *The Hitchhiker* (1953), the wonderful *Suddenly* (1954), and the spooky classics *Carnival of Souls* (1962) and *Night of the Living Dead* (1966).

Occasionally, films landing in the public domain can bring fame to them and their stars who were lost to obscurity. An example is *Detour* (1945). This little B-picture noir is of a genre I don't particularly like: films about lowlife losers who lose. Directed by Edgar Ulmer, a Jewish-Moravian-Austrian-American—yes, you read that right—director who specialized in tragic films made on even sadder budgets (more about him later), the film stars Tom Neal (more about him later) as Al Roberts, a down-on-his-luck piano player hitching his way from New York to Los Angeles to see his girlfriend. He is picked up by a jovial con artist who buys him a meal and tells him about a woman he gave a ride to who had a terrible temper and scratched his hand badly. He likely deserved it.

Anyway, the con artist is popping speed to stay awake for the drive. He lets Al drive and passes out in the passenger seat. Al stops to put up the top of the convertible in a rainstorm, opens the passenger-side door, and out falls the con artist, hitting his head on a rock. Seeing he is dead, Al does what the ancient Greeks termed "exposing his tragic flaw"; instead of calling the police and maybe taking a few bucks out of the guy's wallet for his troubles, our hero changes places with the con artist.

This seems to work fine at first; Al finds himself with a car, a large bankroll, and even nice pajamas to wear in a quiet, clean hotel room. But, alas, our hero has another tragic flaw; he likes to pick up pretty hitchhikers, and soon he picks up Vera, who turns out to be the very same girl the con artist encountered. And what a dame; Vera, played by Ann Savage (more about her later), is an angry, violent, alcoholic, promiscuous consumptive—quite a catch—who knows Al is not who is says he is and accuses him of murder. They get to LA all right but no rendezvous with his girlfriend for Al. Vera blackmails him into renting an apartment, buying her clothes, selling the car, and scheming to claim an inheritance. They get drunk, fight, and it does not end well. Al ends up running—spoiler alert—from *two* murder charges he is innocent of.

In my opinion, this is not a good movie; the acting is wooden, the plot's a real doggie downer, and our hero provides nonstop narration throughout the film that is both inane and unnecessary. It is very easy to imagine a better movie without it. The only purpose of the narration that I can see is to explain the insipid choices Al makes throughout the film.

The irony of the movie is that it's theme of bad choices leading to ruin was mirrored in the real lives of director and star. Ulmer had initial success in German and then US filmmaking, directing the groundbreaking *The Black Cat* in 1934. That film, starring Boris Karloff and Bella Lugosi, was the first of Universal's atmospheric horror films. But, alas, Ulmer's tragic flaws were bad judgment and women; he stole the wife of the nephew of studio mogul Carl Laemmle, and before you could say *detour*, he was sidelined into "ethnic" and Poverty Row films. Maybe the director saw *Detour* as autobiographical. In 1960, he made *Beyond the Time Barrier* for almost nothing in ten days, filming in a park in Texas where the backers lived; see my review of *The Yesterday Machine*. Ulmer made his last cheapie in 1964 and died of a massive stroke eight years later.

Star Tom Neal also had fate turn on him. Starting with a successful boxing career (1932–1934), Neal went on to star in nearly sixty B pictures. His tragic flaws were his temper and women: his first wife divorced him for mental cruelty, he married his second wife after badly beating her boyfriend, and he killed his third wife by shooting her in the head. Similar to *Detour*, he claimed it was not murder but a freak accident, and he went to prison for manslaughter. Neal died in bed of a massive heart attack in 1972, the same year as Ulmer.

Ann Savage fared a little better, although it took the public domain to save her from obscurity. She acted in about twenty B pictures during a ten-year period and then quit the movies to work as an administrative assistant for different companies. All that changed after *Detour* entered the public domain. Suddenly, it was shown to a younger audience on TV and VHS tapes, and by the late 1980s, the film had developed a cult status as a low-budget noir classic. Savage was the darling of film festivals, and in 2005, she was named an "icon and legend" by the Academy of Motion Picture Arts and Sciences. In 2007, *Time Magazine* placed *Detour* on its list of the Top 100 Films of All Time (!) and Savage's portrayal of Vera in the Top 10 Movie Villains of All Time. That same year, she starred in Canadian filmmaker Guy Maddin's tribute to his hometown, *My Winnipeg*. Savage played Maddin's mother, and the movie won Best Feature Film at the Toronto International Film Festival, in addition to other accolades. Savage died a year later, but in 2010 a book chronicle of her film career was published.

Ulmer also had posthumous fame; a revival of his work was held at the thirtieth anniversary of his death, and since 2006, an annual Ulmerfest has been held in Europe to celebrate the director. *Detour* was selected for the US National Film Registry by the Library of Congress as being "culturally, historically, or aesthetically significant."

Wow. I still think *Detour* is a bomb, but what do I know? If you have personally been in a film I think is bad, you can wait for it to go into the public domain thirty years later and prove me wrong, or you can put it on YouTube now and see if it goes viral. A lot of stuff, from great to putrid, does.

King of the Zombies (1941): Back to Basics

Reviewing *Detour* really messed with my head. Was it a bomb? Was it great cinematic art? To clear my confusion, I had to go back to the basics and find a *definite* bomb. A surefire way of doing that is to go back to anything made by good ol' reliable Monogram Pictures.

Monogram Pictures (1931–1953 and then to 1979 as Allied Artists) was one of the Poverty Row studios that made particularly inexpensive B pictures, hundreds of forgettable flops, and some reasonably successful but cheaply made series such as *Bomba the Jungle Boy, Charlie Chan* (after it was dropped by 20th Century Fox), the *Bowery Boys / East End Kids, Cisco Kid, Joe Palooka,* and lesser series like *Snuffy Smith.* At a time when most B pictures cost $600,000 to make, Monogram could grind one out for $90,000 using lesser names, recycled sets and film clips, and black-and-white shooting.

Much of the filming, particularly the short, cheap, but action-packed westerns that got the studio started, was done on Monogram Ranch in the foothills of the northern San Gabriel Mountains. The studio was run from a complex of brick buildings on Sunset Boulevard. Utilizing European film studios, Allied Artists had some success with movies like *Cabaret* (1972), *Papillion* (1973), and *The Man Who Would Be King* (1975). And I am forever grateful to Allied for turning out the greatest low-budget sci-fi film of all time, the previously mentioned *Invasion of the Body Snatchers* (1956). But most of Monogram/Allied's output was junk, so to find comfort in a good bomb, I had only to turn to *King of the Zombies*, a typical Monogram quickie.

In 1941, the hot topics for action movies were spies—done with class the year before in Hitchcock's *Foreign Correspondent*—and zombies, and so this sixty-seven-minute gem features both. The movie opens with a Capelis XC-12 transport plane, another great aircraft—see my review of *Home to Danger*—struggling in a storm. In the original zombie pictures, the term *zombies* meant Blacks in the Caribbean under the spell of voodoo magic, and so the plane is "somewhere between Cuba and Puerto Rico." On board are the pilot, played by Dick Purcell, who finally found success after a long string of B pictures with the Captain America serials, only to drop dead of a massive heart attack in 1944; his friend Bill, played by John Archer, a character actor you have seen in a lot of B movies and on TV; and the great Mantan Moreland, playing Bill's valet, Jeff. Apparently, Bill doesn't go anywhere without his valet.

They are looking for a Coast Guard admiral whose plane went down a week before. Of course, their plane goes down too, and we cut to the wreck. It looks bad, but they look great, their ties and dinner jackets uncreased. The pilot has a band-aid on his forehead, and that's it. It's a good thing they are dressed for dinner because they "stumble"—it's right there—onto a huge mansion filled with elegant-looking people who are also dressed for dinner. And so, they all have dinner. At the head of the table is a doctor named Sangre—look it up if you don't speak Spanish—who is played by character actor Henry Victor. Victor, an English-German-American character actor, appeared in over one hundred B pictures, usually as a "foreigner," and died of a brain tumor in 1945. Here he plays a menacing-looking yet apparently hospitable recluse who does a Bela Lugosi imitation; apparently even Lugosi bowed out of this stinker. Dr. Sangre is interested in voodoo and collects voodoo masks, including a "prized mask from Holland" (!). His wife appears to be under some kind of spell—voodoo, possibly?—but she's still dressed nicely for dinner.

It all results in predictable nonsense involving secret doors, hypnotism, and zombies. Sangre turns out to be an "agent of a foreign power"—his German is awfully good—who is holding the admiral hostage and trying to extract information from him. Does he torture the admiral to get it? No, he tortures the audience by subjecting them to a ridiculous scene where he ties the guy to a chair and stands over him with a voodoo mask while his cook, who is really a voodoo priestess, shouts voodoo chants at him, and all the Black cast members bang on drums and sing something that sounds like "I eat . . . I eat . . . I eat coq au vin!" Apparently, the voodoo priestess and Sangre are trying to use voodoo magic to transfer the admiral's knowledge into the brain of a pretty girl. She is played by Joan Woodbury, whose Danish-British-Indigenous American heritage resulted in her often being cast as a mysterious, "exotic-looking" femme fatale. Behind them stand a bunch of zombies who are apparently ready to do Sangre's evil work.

Bill and Jeff break in on the proceedings and—spoiler alert—for some unexplained reason, the zombies turn on Sangre and back him into a giant fire pit. The admiral is saved, boys get girls, and even the poor pilot, who was hypnotized and shot twice, recovers and is "raring to go" after getting "patched up by the Coast Guard."

The most interesting thing about *King of the Zombies* is that, despite the status of Black actors in Hollywood in 1941, the real star is Moreland. He even gets third billing, behind Purcell and Woodbury and in front of Archer and Victor. Sure, it is understood—and even made light of—that he can't drink with whites, has to live with the other Black servants, and is talked down to by Archer. However, he is the most entertaining and least cardboard character to watch, and even audiences in 1941 may have known that. Moreland was a favorite comedian in the Monogram studio and appeared frequently in its horror/action/mystery films as a valet or chauffeur to add comic relief and insight.

Moreland was often paired with other Black comedians—here, Marguerite Whitten but more often his vaudeville partner, Ben Carter—to provide snappy, humorous dialogue. Moreland is best remembered as chauffeur Birmingham Brown in the Monogram Charlie Chan entries, in which he and Carter do their famous "indefinite talk" routine. The routine involves Moreland and Carter carrying on a conversation by completing each other's sentences; nouns and facts are dropped out, but they act like they understand each other perfectly.

By the 1950s, Moreland's bug-eyed nervous demeanor and Stepin Fetchit delivery had fallen out of favor in movie culture, but Moreland continued to make personal appearances, using younger Black comedians like Redd Foxx and Nipsey Russell as straight men. He was even considered for the role of the third stooge in *The Three Stooges* after Shemp Howard died suddenly in 1955. Columbia chose Joe Besser instead, not because of Moreland's race but because they wanted someone who was already under Columbia contract. Too bad.

Unlike *Detour*, I don't think *King of the Zombies* will be re-discovered by avant-garde film critics, studied at universities, or selected for the US National Film Registry by the Library of Congress as being "culturally, historically, or aesthetically significant." No, even though it was actually nominated for an Academy Award (Best Musical Score) and followed by a sequel, *Revenge of the Zombies* (1943), I think it's status as a bomb is secure.

We have Monogram Pictures to thank for so many bombs. The Monogram Ranch is gone, and the red brick buildings on Sunset Boulevard are now owned by the Church of Scientology, but Monogram lives on in the hearts of true bomb fans like me.

8

The Thirteenth Guest (1932): Outed by the Venn Diagram

In a prior review, I alluded to the fact that finding bombs among certain film genres known to be bad is fairly easy. For example, every bomb hunter knows that any movie made by poor Ed Wood Jr., branded the worst director of all time, is a bomb. So what? Too easy.[1] No, the skilled bomb sleuth uses other tools to find great bombs, such as the Venn diagram. As you hopefully remember from grade-school math, a Venn diagram is a pictorial representation of the intersection of two sets, showing the area that the sets have in common. To find bombs, we simply intersect sets known to contain bombs and find their common factors.

An example: crossing films made by Monogram Pictures with pre-code films. As I mentioned in the prior review, Monogram Pictures was a Poverty Row Hollywood studio that specialized in B pictures. Most were bombs, but some, like *Kidnapped* (1948)

---

1 If you were to talk film with me in person, I may argue that Wood was simply misunderstood and financially handicapped; many directors have done less with far more.

and *Suspense* (1946), were actually pretty good. Pre-code films were movies made between 1929, when most pictures turned talkie, and 1934, when the Production Code Administration (PCA) was established. The Hays Code, which was designed to monitor the moral content of films, was actually created in 1930 but was not really enforced until the creation of the PCA. As a result, from 1929 to 1934, without pressure from censors, films were able to lure audiences with stories involving sex, interracial marriage, profanity, drug use, promiscuity, prostitution, abortion, homosexuality, extreme violence, and—worst of all—evil characters who got away with their crimes. All of these themes were banished from the screen by the PCA, which made sure that entertainment was "clean" and that crime did not pay.

Many pre-code films were decidedly *not* bombs, including *Baby Face* (1933), *The Bitter Tea of General Yen* (1932), *The Black Cat* (1934, mentioned in a previous review), *Dr. Jekyll and Mr. Hyde* (1931), *Employees' Entrance* (1933), *Freaks* (1932), the has-to-be-seen-to-be-believed *Gabriel over the White House* (1934), *Gold Diggers of 1933*, *I Am a Fugitive from a Chain Gang* (1932), *The Lost Patrol* (1934), *Scarface* (1932), *The Sign of the Cross* (1932), *Tarzan and His Mate* (1934), and *Three on a Match* (1932), just to name a few. But do the Venn diagram between Monogram Pictures and pre-code films, and in the intersection, you'll find some nice bombs. Case in point: *The Thirteenth Guest*.

In this sixty-nine-minute creaky bit of nonsense, which, believe it or not, was filmed again in 1943, members of a family named Morgan who attended a dinner party years before are murdered one by one and their bodies placed in the chairs they sat in at the original party. The thirteenth chair at that party was empty, and the police hypothesize that the murderer is the thirteenth guest, who never showed up at the dinner. The main character, Marie Morgan, the youngest person at the dinner, is played by none other than Ginger Rogers, only twenty-one at the time of filming and two years away from "doing it backwards and in heels" for the first time with Fred Astaire in *The Gay Divorcee* (1934). Marie is—here's a stretch—a twenty-one-year-old socialite who just inherited a bunch of money. Looking nothing like she did in her musicals, Ms. Rogers appears here as a real flapper, complete with fur coat, cloche, and no bra.

The murders are investigated by a private detective named Phil Winston, played by the ubiquitous Lyle Talbot. Talbot, a founding member of the Screen Actors Guild, starred in over 150 B pictures before moving on to TV as a character actor best noted for playing Ozzie and Harriet's next-door neighbor, Mr. Randolph. Winston runs rings around the idiot policemen on the case, who mostly supply the comic relief. On the way to the obvious solution, the audience is tortured with the usual Monogram tricks, including secret rooms, phony cobwebs, a mysterious character in a mask and cape, and a diabolic murder device—an electrified telephone. The film even throws in a Depression-era humor bit, done better later in *My Man Godfrey* (1936), in which rich folks are thrown into prison and have to hobnob with lowlifes.

The film is lost dreck that should have stayed buried, but it has some typical pre-code features that are fun to look for: a homosexual character; profanity, like telling someone they can "go to the devil!"—strong stuff in 1932; and mild promiscuity. Every time we see Detective Winston at home, he is with another babe who is drinking with him and may or may not be wearing anything. In the last scene—spoiler alert—the babe is none other than Marie. We see a nice view of Ms. Rogers's décolletage in a low-cut gown, which she subsequently proceeds to drape over Mr. Talbot as she reaches over him for the phone.

Oh, brother, I need to get out more.

9

The Yesterday Machine (1963?, 1965?):
Regional Films and Bad Teeth

As noted in the last review, certain film genres are an obvious and rich source of bombs, such as Sword and Sandal, Blaxploitation, '50s cheapo Sci-Fi, et cetera, et cetera. I feel guilty looking for bombs in these places because it's too easy. But I am not ashamed to delve into regional films occasionally, because few people actually know what they are.

Regional film is a term used to describe movies made in various regions of the United States outside of Hollywood, typically in the 1950s–1970s, often sci-fi or horror. These movies, made long before the term *independent film* was coined, were made by locals in a given community using local talent as well as local film people and equipment and were usually made on low budgets and released to a limited audience.

These were basically vanity projects made by people who wanted to see their names and those of their neighbors up in lights. They usually starred people you never heard of, doing their best despite the fact that most were amateurs. If the budgets were high enough, the filmmakers might have been able to hire a "big star" to give the film some credibility. Some of these films were eventually picked up by distributors and shown more widely, usually in drive-ins or smaller theaters and often as double features with B-picture sci-fi/horror films made by actual Hollywood studios. The audiences understood that these second features were bombs that theater owners used, along with cartoons, newsreels, and ads, to fill time around the main feature. Because regional films began with regional showings and only occasionally were more widely released, it could be hard to assign a single release date to the occasional ones that made it to the big time.

A typical example is *The Yesterday Machine*, with an uncertain release date of either 1963 or 1965. The film was made by some Texas millionaires in the Dallas area using local film crews, writers, and actors and features a local singer and local performers you never heard of. There is even a local baton twirler with nice legs named Linda Jenkins, who opens the film with a several-minute routine. The opening credits then begin and go on for a while, listing all the locals who likely paid into the film to see their names.

The story concerns two modern "kids"—the aforementioned baton twirler and her clean-cut boyfriend, complete with a generic '60s letterman's sweater—who get lost in the woods and encounter two Civil War soldiers. The boy gets shot and makes it to a nearby road before collapsing, but the baton twirler vanishes.

The boy is brought to the hospital (Parkland?), where no one believes his "fantastic story" until the doctor, who just happens to be a collector of Civil War weapons, digs out the bullets and discovers they are genuine Civil War ammo. A search is made of the place where the boy was shot, and only the girl's sweater and a Civil War cap are found. Apparently, the cap is authenticated by the police when they look at the label. Wait . . . what?

Enter reporter Jim Crandall, who interviews the baton twirler's sister, a platinum-blond lounge singer who looks old enough to be the baton twirler's mother. The reporter and the lounge singer are clearly the love story of the film; they begin a search for the baton twirler and, within minutes, are embracing and calling each other by their first names. I guess when a film is only seventy-eight minutes long, you've got to work fast. They are played by people you never heard of, so I won't tell you their names. I will tell you this: they have really bad teeth. I guess good dental care was not a priority in Texas in the '60s.

The makers of the film did spend money to buy one "star": Tim Holt. Holt is an interesting person; he made his early career working for RKO, mostly as a cowboy star, but got a career boost when Orson Welles cast him in *The Magnificent Ambersons* (1942). Along came the war, and Holt, who had a military background, enlisted in the air force and flew in B-29s as a bombardier over Japan, getting wounded and earning a Purple Heart.

Holt returned to movies but now starred in high-budget westerns like *My Darling Clementine* (1946) and films written by the great western writer Zane Grey. In 1949, his career peaked when he was loaned out to Warner Brothers to star opposite Humphrey Bogart and Walter Huston in *The Treasure of the Sierra Madre* (1949). Holt then went back to RKO, where he remained pigeonholed in increasingly less successful westerns, finally quitting the movies and moving to Oklahoma to work in rodeos and as an animal nutritionist and making personal appearances. In 1957, he starred in a B sci-fi film called *The Monster That Challenged the World*, which he actually said was "not bad"; see the next review.

By 1965 or '63, when the Texas millionaires spent a little

coin to have Holt be their star in *The Yesterday Machine*, he looked old and very tired. Holt played the detective who works with the reporter and the lounge singer to find the baton twirler. He has exactly four scenes, but one is a diatribe where he tells the reporter that in the war, his squadron liberated a concentration camp full of healthy-looking young people and a mad scientist named Von Hauser, who had a "weird machine" in one of the buildings. Von Hauser and the machine disappeared. The silly plot, the farfetched connection between the girl's disappearance and evil Nazi time travelers, and the fact that the detective investigating the case just happens to link it all together with some of the worst dialogue ever written make this cheapo bomb a real gem. And, oh yeah, Tim Holt has really bad teeth too.

The only person in the movie who has nice teeth, which are probably dentures, is the scrawny, weird-looking actor—someone else you never heard of—who plays Von Hauser. Oh yeah, the reporter and lounge singer stumble on an old house that houses Herr Von Hauser—say that three times fast; his time machine, which consists of a wooden chair surrounded by four poles with flashing lights; a dungeon; two evil Nazi stooges; and—wait for it—an Egyptian princess. The most amazing thing about the movie is that when Von Hauser captures our heroes, he does not torture or kill them. No, he gives them a *twenty-minute*—I'm not kidding; I timed it—chalk talk about time travel. It's the stupidest movie pseudo-science you ever heard, so I guess Von Hauser *was* torturing someone: the audience. This film never made it much past Texas drive-ins until it found a wider audience on VHS release, so I guess Von Hauser's speech was when people went to the refreshment center.

Anyway, our heroes—spoiler alert—rescue the baton twirler, escape, and Holt shows up and destroys the time machine. The film was incredibly cheaply made, filmed on video with a terrible improvised jazz score so common to this crap—think *Little Shop of Horrors* (1960)—and using cheap sets at the Studio Recording Center in Dallas.

There is an interesting background to bombs like *The Yesterday Machine*: the Texas millionaires who financed it were likely ex-GIs who came back from the war with battle fatigue, wrapped in fears that the Nazis (a) would have won had they developed the "super weapons," such as the Nazi equivalent of the H bomb, that were widely rumored to be in development at the end of the war and (b) that the Third Reich was in hiding and would rise again. These very real fears were fodder for Z-grade sci-fi films of the '60s, a genre I may return to in a future review—as soon as I get my time machine up and working.

10

The Monster That Challenged the World (1957): What's in a Name?

What's in a name? When it comes to movies, a lot. Some films started out with really terrible working titles: *A Boy's Life* became *E.T.*, *Everybody Comes to Rick's* became *Casablanca*, *A Long Night at Camp Blood* became *Friday the 13th*, and *Stand by Me* started out named for the Stephen King story it's based on, *The Body*. Hitchcock's greatest film, with the greatest title, *Psycho*, started out with a wimpy title: they actually wanted to call it *Wimpy*. *Alien* was almost called *Star Beast*. *When I Grow Up* was retitled *Big*.

Oftentimes studios recognize that the working title was just too long. *The Tribal Rites of New Saturday Night* was retitled *Saturday Night Fever*, and *How the Solar Space Race Was Won* was renamed *2001: A Space Odyssey*. Sometimes the titles are just too terrible; *Annie Hall* was originally called *It Had to Be Jew*—no joke. *The Cut Whore Killings* was released as *Unforgiven*.

As you can see, studios often replace working titles with new titles that are shorter / punchier / less ridiculous. The opposite happened with a 1957 low-budget sci-fi film originally titled *The Kraken*. Prior to release, United Artists actually retitled it *The Monster That Challenged the World*. There are so many things wrong with that title it's hard to list them all. But let me try.

First, it has too many syllables: nine. It's hard to think of good films with that many syllables in the tile. I can think of two: *The Taking of Pelham 1-2-3* (1974, 2009) and *The St. Valentine's Day Massacre* (1967). Even the not-so-good and incorrectly named *Krakatoa, East of Java* (1968) had only eight. Krakatoa is west of Java.

Secondly, there is that word *challenged*. Monsters threaten, attack, and kill people, yes, but challenge them, no. *Challenged* sounds like a boxing match. "In this corner, weighing in at 6×10^{21} tons, the world! And in this corner, weighing 1 ton, the monster!"

Thirdly, there's that word *monster*. And what monster would that be? The kraken? No, the movie ended up not being about the kraken, which is why they had to change the working title. A kraken, as any sea-farin' bloke knows, is a mythical giant squid that attacked ships in days of yore. No, the makers of this film apparently could not even afford the rubber octopus that Bella Lugosi wrestled with in *Bride of the Monster* (1955) and certainly not the wonderful mechanical giant squid in Disney's *20,000 Leagues under the Sea* (1954). So the "monster" in this film is a—wait for it—giant snail. Snails, as you know, are not fast, so the victims in this horror film have to stand still and scream while the snail slowly attacks them—an old movie gimmick so wonderfully lampooned in *Austin Powers, International Man of Mystery* (1997).

More correctly, these are snails—grammar nerds will note that the title also contains a plurality error—that live in the bottom of the Salton Sea in California. Their presence is suggested by papier-mâché shells and eggs that look a lot like beach balls. Shot for $200K in 16 days, the film is mostly stock footage, rear-screen projection, outdoor filming around the California Aqueduct, underwater shots of divers around Catalina, and close-ups of the actors with their heads in fish tanks, wearing scuba masks and behind fake seaweed. The professor—a rare "serious" role played by Hans Conried—gives a lecture to the navy security troops on mollusks that actually utilizes a high school movie about snails and an article in *Life* magazine.

Tim Holt once again came out of retirement to play the leading role of the security chief of a supposed naval base on the Salton Sea, which is surprising, given how shallow it was even then—see my review of *Highway Dragnet*. Toward the end of his career, there were apparently few films Holt wouldn't come out of retirement for; see my review of *The Yesterday Machine*. He romances Audrey Dalton, a fairly pretty Irish actress. Holt was fifteen years her senior; I had to look it up since he looks more than thirty years older than her, and their scenes together are creepier than the giant snails. Another interesting face in the cast is Max Showalter, a ubiquitous character actor I best remember as the husband who rescues his wife from the falls in the Marilyn Monroe film *Niagara* (1953) and in the creepy *Twilight Zone* episode "It's a Good Life" with Billy Mumy. Here he plays a navy frogman who is quite shaken after he sees his pal slowly eaten by one of the snails. The great Milton Parsons, who always played creepy skinny guys with a weird smile, plays a creepy skinny guy with a weird smile.

Back to the title. A fourth problem with it is the term *world*. In the end—spoiler alert—the monsters don't get past the Salton Sea. So, it seems, a more accurate title for this bomb would have been *The Giant Snails That Challenged the Salton Sea*, but who would see a movie with that title? Besides, it has an intolerable twelve syllables.[2]

The title *The Monster That Challenged the World* has six words, and I have taken issue with four of them. Let me take issue with a fifth word: *that*. As a woke reviewer,[3] I want to know if anyone asked the monster what its preferred pronoun was. Did anyone let the monster self-identify? *That* implies that the monster's preferred pronoun was *it*, but what if their preferred pronoun was *she*, *he*, or even *they*? In *that* case, the monster's correct pronoun for the title would be *who*. I think this microaggression against giant snails must stop.

On a positive note, I have no objections to the word *the* in the title.

---

2   The astute reader will note that I have not taken my own advice; the title of this book has twenty-four syllables. Unforgivable.

3   Just kidding; see Preface.

11

Jail Bait (1954): Did Ed Wood Make a Film That Was *Not* a Bomb?

It's so easy to make fun of poor Ed Wood. Ever since winning a Golden Turkey Award and being declared the worst director of all time, people have been laughing at Wood's sad film work for decades. Finally, in 1994, Tim Burton made *Ed Wood*, a partial biopic that focused on the making of *Bride of the Monster* (1955), the one where Bela Lugosi wrestles with a rubber octopus; see my prior review. Burton actually managed to capture Wood's enthusiasm for filmmaking, his affection for and support of the studio of misfit "actors" he had assembled, and the rather creative ways he managed to make films on nonexistent budgets. Ironically, Burton's film about the maker of terrible films made a bunch of money and won two Academy Awards.

As a scientist, I asked myself a simple scientific question: Did Wood ever make a good film, one that was *not* a bomb? If you view his career as consisting of three parts, there are two possibilities: the two films that transitioned each part. In the first part of his career, Wood was just trying to break into movies and did anything and everything it took—he wrote, acted, made TV pilots, and even did stunts. In this part of his career, he directed one film, the notorious *Glen or Glenda* (1953), a pseudo-documentary about transvestitism. The second part of his career was mainly marked by his now-infamous science fiction trilogy, the aforementioned *Bride of the Monster* (1955), *Night of the Ghouls* (1958), and, of course, *Plan 9 from Outer Space* (1959). The third part of his career was basically ruin; Wood slipped into making exploitation films and pornography. By 1978, Wood and his wife, Kathy, had become penniless alcoholics, and Wood died after a weekend of vodka binge-drinking.

The "swing films" between the three parts of his career seemed to me to be the best places to look for a non-bomb. Indeed, those two films seemed to be the ones taken most seriously by critics. Between parts two and three, Wood made *The Sinister Urge*, an exploitation film about a link between murdering women and watching pornography. Nah. That left only the film Wood made between parts one and two, a crime story entitled *Jail Bait* (1954), also known as *The Hidden Face*.

On the surface, there is hope for this film. It was actually produced and released theatrically; it made money, has a soundtrack, and contains a musical number by an actual performer; it features a cast of recognizable names, has a car chase, and has been called a crime film noir. Like many such films of the '40s and '50s, *Jail Bait* features a gangster trying to escape justice through plastic surgery. It received two positive reviews. So . . . is *Jail Bait* a bomb?

Let's get real; of course it is. Taking apart the above arguments for non-bombness, one at a time: First, yes, it was released—by a company called Howco, formed by two guys who reportedly cheated Wood out of his share of the small profit it made running mostly in theaters in the Deep South, which accounts for the musical number. The producers inserted a clip of a Blackface performer named Cotton Watts doing his act on a stage in Florida. It's quite insulting by today's standards, but the guy danced, ironically, like Michael Jackson. As for the musical score, it consists of someone banging on a piano and strumming flamenco guitar. It runs without any pattern through the movie, and it's incredibly annoying.

Yes, the cast has some recognizable folks; the ubiquitous Lyle Talbot—see my review of *The Thirteenth Guest*—plays the detective. Talbot had a long and busy career, apparently because there was no role he wouldn't accept. He "starred" in three Ed Wood films, the others being *Glen or Glenda* (1953) and *Plan 9 from Outer Space* (1959). His partner is played by a young Steve Reeves before he went off to Italy to play Hercules. This is a rare opportunity to hear Reeves speak in his own voice. It isn't bad, but his role is totally disposable.

The two detectives chase after a gangster, played by Timothy Farrell—more about him in the next review. The gangster's girlfriend is played by model Theodora Thurman, who was a sultry-voiced Lauren Bacall lookalike. She never made it in the movies—this was her only film—but she found fame as weather girl Miss Monitor on the radio. The gangster is blackmailing a plastic surgeon, played by Herbert Rawlinson. Rawlinson had been a silent screen star, but his career tanked with the advent of talking pictures. Too bad. His voice is not bad, but he's hard to listen to because he had terminal lung cancer and died the very night he finished his scenes. You can hear him struggling to catch his breath between lines.

Even more painful than listening to Rawlinson deliver those lines are the lines themselves. Written by Wood and his writing partner, Alex Gordon, their script contains the usual silly dialogue and weird non sequiturs: the surgeon muses that surgery can sometimes be complicated, and a gangster's moll notes that she was told not to take chances, so that's "just what (she's) going to do." With the exception of Talbot, Rawlinson, and possibly Ferrell, the lines are delivered in a wooden style by "actors" with little to no experience: Wood's girlfriend, Dolores Fuller, "stars" in her second film, after *Glen or Glenda*, and her dramatic skills have not improved. And speaking of no acting experience, the main character, the plastic surgeon's son, is played by Wood's grocery boy, Clancy Malone. As the saying goes, Malone told Wood that he wanted to be in a movie "in the worst way," and that is exactly what happened to Malone when he appeared in *Jail Bait*. Not surprisingly, this was his one and only film credit. Ironically, Clancy, playing a good boy gone bad, shoots and kills a security guard played by the most seasoned player in the whole mess—Bud Osborn, a character actor who appeared in over six hundred films and TV shows.

Although *Jail Bait* has a been called a film noir, I think it has been *mistaken* for a film noir because all the scenes occur at night. That is likely because filming in the dark saved the filmmakers from using any scenery, hiring extras, or having to show anything outside the windows. Speaking of film noir, Lauren Bacall, and plastic surgery, *Jail Bait* is sometimes erroneously compared to *Dark Passage* (1947), a Bogart-Bacall movie that is perhaps one thousand times better. But not nearly as—unintentionally—funny.

Girl Gang (1954): Not Just a Bomb

In a previous review, I said that I would not look for bombs among certain genres, including exploitation films, because it was just too easy. Boy, am I sorry I went back on that promise.

It was my fault; after seeing *Jail Bait*, I wanted to see Timothy Farrell in action because I just couldn't believe this guy. Did he really make a career playing such nasty characters? What was he like in real life?

Well, the answer to the first question is yes. He acted in some really bad stuff for Z-grade producer George Weiss, as well as such classics as *Test Tube Babies* (1948) and *Glen or Glenda* (1953). In 1954, he had a banner year with *Jail Bait* and a stinker called *Girl Gang*. He usually played evil doctors and criminals, and in *Girl Gang*, he plays a character he played in other films, "Joe the Pimp."

As you may have guessed, Joe is not a nice guy. He operates a gang of female thieves out of his house and then gets them hooked on drugs, marijuana and heroin, which he sells them after they split up the money from their capers so he can take their share away right after he gives it to them. The rather old-looking high school girls in his gang talk tough and deliver their ridiculous lines in a wooden style that would have made me laugh if it wasn't for the sheer nastiness of the film. In sixty-one minutes—actually fifty-one; ten minutes are wasted watching kids dance while some guy bangs on a piano—the film manages to squeeze in catfights, prostitution, shootouts, and *lots* of drug use, including a step-by-step primer delivered by Joe on how to mainline heroin.

Joe's girlfriend, June, played by Playboy model Joanne Arnold, has it rough; she steals and prostitutes herself for him, while he gets her hooked on heroin. The whole film is really an excuse to see women in their underwear; June hitches up her skirt to get a shot in the thigh and takes off her dress to seduce her lecherous boss. When one woman is shot, the audience is treated to an emergency bullet removal from her chest, which consists mostly of the other actors tearing off her blouse.

Compared to *Jail Bait*, *Girl Gang* is a lavish extravaganza; there is a soundtrack, and scenes are filmed during the day with actual extras and real scenery, including a block of '50s LA that looks like the same low-rent housing featured in *He Walked by Night*—see my review. But while *Jail Bait* was stupid, it wasn't sleazy. That primer on mainlining is actually repeated in *Girl Gang* a couple more times during the fifty-one minutes, just in case the audience didn't get all the details the first time. *Girl Gang* is one of those pieces of schlock that makes you want to take a bath when it's done to wash off the smell. I'm dropping this kind of exploitation film again; *Girl Gang* is not just a bomb—it's a stink bomb.

As to my second question—what was Timothy Farrell like in real life?—well, ironically, he made these films to supplement his job as a bailiff for the LA County Marshal's office. He also had one respectable role: he played a bailiff—that was a stretch—in George Cukor's *A Star Is Born* (1954). An early animal rights advocate and a World War II Army Air Corp Veteran, Farrell actually was eventually elected LA County Marshal. A good guy, right?

But, alas, life *does* imitate art: Farrell was fired after committing a felony in office. This was not the first time he had been in jail; he was caught in a vice raid making an exploitation film called *Paris after Midnight* (1951). That one I am *definitely* going to skip.

A Tale of Two Bombs, Part 1: *Phantom Planet* (1961)

Like all nerds, I enjoy the banter of *Mystery Science Theater 3000* (*MST3000*). Watching the human and his two robot sidekicks make fun of really bad movies can be hilarious. Yet I feel a little guilty when I watch that show. The wooden acting, terrible scripts, unknown actors, bad special effects, and low production values of a good bomb should stand alone as the hallmarks of a bomb, and real bomb aficionados should enjoy them for what they are and respect those features when they find them, not ridicule them.

When *MST3000* first came out, it attacked the really *bad* films that are out there, like *The Robot vs. the Aztec Mummy* (1958; season 1, episode 2). By season 4, episode 16, *MST* found *Fire Maidens from Outer Space* (*FMFOS*; 1956). This film and the ones that preceded it were fairly low-hanging fruit as bad films go. However, I couldn't help noticing that a film often paired with *FMFOS*, 1961's *Phantom Planet*, was not noticed by *MST3000* until the ninth season. This made me wonder if *Phantom Planet* was really that bad or if it was unfairly picked on just a year before *MST3000* ended, not counting the Netflix revival.

So I took a look. *Phantom Planet* begins with a nutty prologue showing stock footage of atom bomb tests from the '40s and '50s with narration that tells the viewer that because of the wonderful atomic energy of today, humans in the future went on to develop rocket bases on the moon by 1980 from which the United States could explore the "distant reaches of space." We cut to a very cheap-looking rocket set and two guys in X-15-like flight suits, whose rocket is drawn toward and crashes on a meteorite, something that looks exactly like a giant honey nut cluster. We then cut to a moon base, where gravity is normal, the walls are lined with the same lights and gauges seen in the spaceship from the previous scene, and people strut around in military uniforms instead of space gear. A general is complaining about losing rockets on the titular Phantom Planet, the honey nut cluster, while his aide expresses frustration by raising his arms all the time without bending his elbows.

The general sends out his ace pilot, Captain Frank Chapman, to find out what is going on with the honey nut cluster. Chapman is played by one of the most Aryan actors I have ever seen, a guy named Dean Fredericks. Fredericks was so white-looking that he was typecast playing very white people, like Jungle Jim and Steve Canyon. Fredericks looks a lot like Harry Carey Jr. and a surgeon I know.

Anyway, Chapman blasts off with a waste-O red shirt named Makonnen; I kept thinking the guy's name was Meconium— look it up. You know Makonnen is doomed when he makes a speech about all the goodness in the universe. Anyway, they both go outside the spaceship to fix something, where there is apparently normal gravity and temperature, sound, and steam; they are still wearing only the X-15 suits. While the writers of this thing did not know much about conditions in space, they did believe that space is filled with dangerous bulletlike particles that whizz by. These things go shooting by our heroes and manage to sever *both* their air hoses. Makonnen manages to stuff an unconscious Chapman into the spaceship before he floats off to that doom I predicted, reciting the Lord's Prayer. It's a nice touch but scientifically impossible because he has no air.

Anyway, our hero then proceeds to pass out not once but three more times, during which the viewer learns that the honey nut cluster is a planet called Rheyton, home to six-inch little men all dressed like extras in *West Side Story* who even scatter and race about in choreographed fashion in fear of the giant Captain Chapman. But once he breathes the air on Rheyton, Chapman shrinks to their size and is captured. Taken back to their underground headquarters—all the sets for this part of the film are basically fake rock walls—Chapman learns that there are also little women, all dressed in '60s women's college tennis dresses, except for two, one blonde and one brunette, who are special because they are dressed in cocktail dresses.

They are Liara and Zetha, respectively. Liara is played by Colleen Gray, who actually starred in some very good films, including Stanley Kubrick's *The Killing* (1956), one of my favorite movies. Zetha is played by a rather unfortunate actress, Delores Faith, who had a striking resemblance to Elizabeth Taylor, especially because she dyed her blond hair dark to match her Italian-Hungarian olive skin. Warner Brothers would apparently not place her under contract because of the resemblance but no matter—as a blonde, the studio thought she resembled Grace Kelly too much, so she couldn't win. Anyway, after a few other low-budget films and some TV work, she married a millionaire, left show business, and died from an apparent suicide. Money really doesn't buy happiness.

The leader of all these little men and women is a very wise-looking older guy who walks around in something that looks like a bathrobe, saying very wise things, including stuff about "life clocks." Look closely—he is none other than Francis X. Bushman. As a young man, Bushman was declared "the Handsomest Man in Hollywood" and "King of the Movies" before Clark Gable. Bushman was a true matinee idol who starred in hundreds of silent films, most notably as Messala in the original *Ben Hur* (1925). As he grew older, Bushman played older sage characters but unfortunately ended his 435-film career with *Phantom Planet*, followed by the stinker *The Ghost in the Invisible Bikini* (1966), the last and the worst of the *Beach Party* films.

Anyway, what follows is a jumble of love triangles, a mute girl who can suddenly speak when the *man she loves* is threatened, an escaped rubber monster, and a "daring" rescue. The thing actually ends—spoiler alert—with that tired gimmick of "The Beginning" being flashed on the screen. The kinder viewer can actually see some elements of this cheapo that remind one of better films such as *Star Wars* (1977) and *This Island Earth* (1955). The latter was actually a pretty good film with a score of 73 percent fresh on Rotten Tomatoes but was nonetheless inexplicably ridiculed in *The MST3000 Movie* (1996).

Phantom Planet is a nice, comfortable bomb; it won't change your life, but it won't make you wish you had the viewing time added back to your life clock.

FMFOS, on the other hand . . .

14

A Tale of Two Bombs, Part 2:
Fire Maidens from Outer Space (1956)

As I mentioned in the previous review, *Fire Maidens from Outer Space (FMFOS)* was picked on much earlier by *Mystery Science Theater 3000 (MST3000)* than *Phantom Planet* (1961), so naturally I had to take a look. I used the opposite reason to look at *Phantom Planet*. Obviously I don't need much of an excuse to view a bomb. Also, some critics have labeled *FMFOS* the "worst movie ever made." Of course, that honor is more often awarded to *Plan 9 from Outer Space* (1959) or any other movie made by Ed Wood, but, regardless, there was a challenge I couldn't pass up. Besides, having already seen *Phantom Planet*, I needed to follow through.

All I can say is that *Phantom Planet* and *FMFOS* would make a great double feature. Both are based on terrible science, both are cheaply made, both feature a bevy of young women in short skirts, both feature actors who had done much better stuff, and both take themselves very seriously.

But to be fair to the science in *FMFOS*, the movie was made in 1956, and while that was a year very dear to this reviewer, it was also the year before Sputnik, and very little was actually known about space travel. Thus, we have five "astronauts," guys in casual military clothing, sitting around a table chain smoking—the prop man must have bought a carton of Chesterfields for the film because everyone, and I mean everyone, smokes the same brand—while their rocket blasts off. No g-force or nothing. As for their spaceship, it is just stock footage of a V-2 rocket superimposed against a black screen with blinking light bulbs for space shots and against a picture of a forest to show a landing.

The reason for the mission is sorta explained in the boring beginning; the five guys are being sent to explore the thirteenth moon of Jupiter. The audience is told that the journey will take three weeks, which the director speeds up by showing a few scenes of the men sharing an electric razor, eating muffins, sleeping, and, of course, smoking Chesterfields. There is normal gravity in space, and thanks to the razor, everyone looks pretty well groomed when they get to their destination and walk outside. Just before they leave the ship, one of the men looks at a gauge and announces that the temperature and air are the same as Earth, which is good since they didn't bring any space suits.

There is a tremendous amount of leering in the film: Early on, the two men in charge of the expedition are at an observatory, where they are mostly observing a secretary—well, that was still the term in 1956—who climbs down a ladder, takes about ten seconds of dictation, and climbs back up, giving them a full minute of running time to leer at her. After they land, the whole crew leers at a statue of a naked woman, and soon they get to leer at a young inhabitant of the planet who is wearing a flimsy costume with a really short skirt. She leads the men to a walled-off civilization inhabited by lots more women in the same costume, and more leering ensues. The women do a poorly choreographed dance to "Stranger in Paradise." Where the music comes from or how these women on a moon of Jupiter got ahold of the opera *Prince Igor* remains unexplained, but by this point, all the men in the audience in 1956 were probably too busy leering to care. There is even a scene filmed at knee height where all the women walk by the camera so the viewer can see their legs.

Anyway, an old man appears and tells the astronauts that this is the lost civilization of Atlantis and that he is the father of all these women. Yeah, right. It seems that the old man and these young women are doing OK; they dance while he drinks grog, wears a toga, and leers at them, and life is good.

But, alas, there is a monster lurking outside the wall. The astronauts soon encounter the monster and learn that the cap guns the prop guy purchased from a toy store—you could buy them anywhere in the '50s—after he bought the carton of Chesterfields, are useless against him. Only the gas bombs the astronauts also carry, something they somehow knew they needed instead of space suits, seem to hold the monster off; I decided to avoid jokes about gas bombs and this movie, but I guess I just made one. The stories you may have heard about this monster are true: he is played by a skinny guy in black clothing wearing a rubber monster mask. Yes, you can actually see the zipper on the front of his black suit, and toward the end of the movie—spoiler alert—you can see the mattress he lands on when he falls into a fire pit spring up on the left of the screen.

It's amazing the connections you can make between bombs. The leader of the astronauts is played by Anthony Dexter, who played the nemesis-turned-comrade of Dean Fredericks in *Phantom Planet*, which also starred Francis X. Bushman. Both Dexter and Bushman were in much better movies and also starred together in a very weird film called *The Story of Mankind* (1957), in which Dexter played Christopher Columbus, and Bushman played Moses. That gives you an idea of what kind of movie it was.

Anyway, back to *FMFOS*. The monster polishes off the old man, the one bad fire maiden, and himself, creating a happy ending where Dexter gets to blast off back to Earth with the lead fire maiden, played by Susan Shaw. Shaw was an English actress—this film was a joint US-English film—who actually had a pretty good career before hitting the skids and dying of cirrhosis in Soho. Alas, there are far fewer happy endings in real life than in the movies. That's part of why I like to lose myself in the pleasures of a good bomb like *FMFOS*.

I conclude that *FMFOS* is not the worst movie ever made. There are films out there that were made with bigger budgets and are much more painful to watch. *FMFOS* is silly escapist fluff that is fun to watch. In fact, I think I'll watch it again to check out that knee-level shot more closely.[4]

---

4 In the interest of full disclosure, I stole this joke, with some paraphrasing, from Roger Ebert.

15

Sabaka (1954): Rocky the Flying Squirrel as a Femme Fatale!

As I've said before, it's amazing the things you can learn and the connections between media you can make when you watch a lot of bombs; at least that's the excuse I use. An example: *Sabaka*. This film is about India in the 1950s, and it is seriously imperialistic. The writers were obviously hooked on Kipling; the story involves a poor boy who does jobs for a rich benefactor (can you say *Kim*?), befriends wild animals (can you say *Jungle Book*?), and is named Gunga Ram. No kidding.

The film was produced by Frank Ferrin, a B-movie and TV producer who produced a mid-'50s TV show called *Andy's Gang*, which featured Andy Devine and showed films like this and shorter TV adventures starring a kid named Nino Marcel, not Indian, as Gunga Ram. Ferrin boasted that although he made only B pictures, he never made a bad one, but judging by this film, I'm not so sure. The dubbing and sound are terrible, it's filmed in a nauseating yellow-green technicolor, and the action and editing are disjointed and hard to follow. It's the kind of films that is so difficult to watch that you feel like you should earn a t-shirt for sitting through its long seventy-eight minutes. I've never seen *Andy's Gang* (and it *is* on YouTube), but judging by this film, it must have been quite the ordeal.

The movie opens with a credit boasting that it was filmed in India due to the kind hospitality of some maharajah, but that is not exactly true. The film consists of scene after scene of stock footage from India, which was likely sent to Ferrin by the maharajah, intermixed with the American cast acting in close-up sets designed to match the stock footage so that it *appears* that the cast and crew went to India. In fact, I don't think they went any farther than Culver City. Some of the film mixing is quite clever—look for scenes involving tree climbing and sword swallowing.

The cast is somewhat notable but seriously wasted. Nino has most of the lines and character development, which makes sense since this is essentially a children's film, while the better-known actors have little to do. Lou Krugman, a busy TV character actor frequently seen on *I Love Lucy*, plays the kindly but temperamental maharajah. Gunga Ram works for him as a *mahout* (elephant rider). The maharajah's constantly around guest from England, Sir Cedric, is played by Reginald Denny, the great aviator, boxer, and war hero. Denny smiles a lot and has exactly one line. Victor Jory—see my review of *Cat-Women of the Moon*—has one scene as a bad guy who is quickly polished off. The biggest name in the cast, Boris Karloff, plays a general who stands around and scoffs at Gunga Ram. He has exactly four scenes and three lines. You can do the math. Vito Scotti—yes, Vito Scotti—plays a nervous neighbor of Gunga's and has more lines than Karloff.

Gunga Ram is quite the guy. He finds a lost elephant cub and rescues a baby from a forest fire, and that's just in the first ten minutes. Thanks to the frantic editing, the actual plot is hard to follow but has something to do with a phony priestess and her henchman who trick the locals in the maharajah's land into worshipping a fire-breathing statue of a supposed fire god named Sabaka; the maharajah notes he has never heard of such a god. The gang is hoping to fleece the people of their belongings by spreading fear and starting fires, one of which kills Gunga's sister and brother-in-law. That turns the movie into a revenge story where Gunga goes after the bad guys.

So why did I suffer through this dreck? Why, to see June Foray, of course! Who, you ask, is June Foray? Only the busiest and most recognizable cast member. How, you ask, is that possible with Boris Karloff in the cast? Well, I answer, you may not recognize June Foray's face, but you have heard her voice thousands of times in countless versions and venues. Foray was perhaps the best-known female voice actor of all time. Chuck Jones, director of the best Warner Brother's Looney Toons cartoons, famously remarked that "June Foray is not the female Mel Blanc, but rather Mel Blanc is the male June Foray." In her nearly eighty-year career in radio and cartoons, Foray played such well-known and beloved characters as Rocky the Flying Squirrel—yes, like Bart Simpson, Rocky was voiced by a female—Natasha, Nell Fenwick, Granny in the "Sylvester and Tweety" cartoons, Cindi Lou Who, all the cackling female characters in *Fractured Fairy Tales*, all the female parts in the great *Stan Freberg Show* (1957), and hundreds of other characters.

Despite this remarkable portfolio, Foray acted in only one live-action film: she plays the evil priestess in *Sabaka*. So, I watched this movie for a chance to see Rocky the Flying Squirrel as a femme fatale, dressed in a G-rated harem costume and spouting commands at flunkies in turbans and oversized diapers. Turns out that when she and her sinister gang finally confront Gunga—spoiler alert—they are no match for his oratory and loyal jungle animals, but no matter. It's fun to see a young Foray using her own voice and chewing the scenery, despite the fact that watching the film is a bit of an effort.

The movie leaves you wondering if Foray could have been a successful live-action actress had she been offered better material and roles. But it was not to be; Foray's career was focused on being heard but not seen. In her later years, Foray became an advocate for animation preservation and, in so doing, preserved much of her own great work.

Each week on the *Rocky and Bullwinkle Show*, Rocky famously introduced upcoming attractions as something you would "really like." I don't think Rocky was referring to *Sabaka*, but the film is definitely a curio.

16

The Last Woman on Earth (1960): Control, Existentialism, Roger Corman, and Puerto Rico

As every film geek knows, if Ed Wood had possessed business savvy, knew what audiences wanted, and made better connections, he would have been Roger Corman.

The now-ninety-seven-year-old Corman started out in the mailroom at 20th Century Fox, rose to script reader and then writer, but left when he felt he was not getting enough credit for his work. He eventually sold his first script, *Highway Dragnet* (1953)—see my review—and used the money to produce his first film, *Monster from the Ocean Floor* (1954). Over the next five decades, Corman produced 385 films and directed 55. He knew how to make films fast and cheap, yet he also knew what audiences liked. Working at the fringes, or completely outside, of Hollywood, the Pope of Pop Cinema helped start the careers of many who would otherwise have been thwarted by the traditional studio systems, including directors Francis Ford Coppola, Ron Howard, Martin Scorsese, Jonathan Demme, Peter Bogdanovich, Joe Dante, John Sayles, and James Cameron; actors Peter Fonda, Jack Nicholson, Dennis Hopper, Bruce Dern, Sylvester Stallone, Diane Ladd, William Shatner; and numerous authors and writers. The guy founded multiple film companies, was hailed by the French New Wave, and has won honorary Academy Awards. Not bad for a guy who—let's face it—has made more bombs than an American munitions factory during World War II.

One of the most obvious keys to the man's success was his pure energy and productivity. Stanley Kubrick took four hundred days to shoot *Eyes Wide Shut*. In fact, Kubrick began the project in 1996 and finished the film in 1999. In contrast, in 1960, Corman and a film crew took a trip to Puerto Rico, where he had discovered there were tax incentives, and made *three* movies over a period of a few weeks, working with essentially five American actors and using Puerto Rican natives for most of the other parts. The three films were made on skeletal budgets; released by his own company, Filmgroup; and made tidy profits.

Corman actually planned to make only two films. The first, *The Battle of Blood Island*, was essentially an antiwar film, based on a story by Phillip Roth, about two World War II GIs who survive an unsuccessful assault of a Japanese-held Pacific island, hide out, and become friends. The audience thinks they are going to sneak up on and attack the small squad of Japanese soldiers holding the island, but just as they are getting ready to do so—spoiler alert—the Japanese commit *hari-kari*. Seems the two GIs were on the island so long they did not hear about the atom bomb and the Japanese surrender. Made for $44,000, Corman called it "a good little picture."

The second film, however, is of much more interest to your humble bomb reviewer. *The Last Woman on Earth* has your typical Corman exploitation title (note that it's not called *The Last*

Two Men on Earth) and your typical Corman titillation poster (featuring a semi-naked woman and the caption "They Fought for the Ultimate Prize!"), but it is not your typical Corman bomb, for several reasons.

First, the production values and music are actually pretty good. The typical Corman choppy sound and editing are gone, and the film, which is in color, is relatively smooth and easy to watch. Gone, too, are the usual cheap sets—think *Little Shop of Horrors*, also made in 1960 but shot in two days and one night. Thanks to my Puerto Rican wife, I have been to Puerto Rico at least a half-dozen times, and I recognized a lot of great location shooting, including the Caribe Hilton, El Morro, and the Church of Santa Maria Reina at Catholic University in Ponce.

The story is intriguing: Harold Gurn and his wife, Evelyn, are vacationing in Puerto Rico—he actually pronounces it *Port-oh Rick-oh*. Harold is a hang-loose, rule-breaking, shady businessman who is having a great time drinking, watching cock fights—the film includes actual graphic scenes of such a fight; it is not for the animal rights advocate—and gambling while ignoring Evelyn. Harold's straitlaced lawyer, Martin, shows up, complete with suit and tie in the Caribbean heat, and begs Harold to forgo the vacation while they review financial briefs to fight an upcoming indictment. Gurn, ever the party boy, goes off to gamble, leaving Martin to discover that Evelyn is depressed and considering suicide. Martin talks her down off a ledge, and Evelyn realizes that Martin, unlike the loutish Harold, can recite poetry, be clever and romantic, and, most of all, listen to her.

Martin keeps after Harold to take the indictment seriously, but Harold responds by coercing Martin into going scuba diving with him and the beautiful Evelyn. While they are underwater breathing oxygen from their tanks, something happens to the world's air, and the oxygen temporarily disappears, killing everyone. They resurface to find that they are the only people left alive in Puerto Rico, possibly the entire world.

The film moves along quickly for its mere sixty-one-minute running time. The three flee to a nice house on the ocean that Harold knows about, and an awkward love triangle forms. That's predictable, but what is not predictable is that the two men change attitudes. Harold becomes uptight and controlling, making "the plan" to stay alive by fishing, learning about food preservation, and avoiding the inevitable insect infestations by constantly moving north to colder weather. Both Martin and Evelyn tell Harold they never agreed to the plan, but he doesn't care, underscoring what a controlling figure he has become.

Conversely, Martin shuns his old—and Harold's new—straitlaced ways, noting that religion, money, and society are gone, and begins to espouse existential thinking. To Martin, Harold's marriage certificate means nothing in their post-apocalyptic world, and he starts to romance Evelyn. In short, the two have completely switched their philosophies of life. In the end—spoiler alert—Harold beats up Martin in a long chase-fight scene, and Martin dies in a church, blinded by head injuries, in Evelyn's arms. The potential symbolism is endless. And, yes, Evelyn goes off with the controlling and abusive Harold.

If you have been following my math, you'll note that Corman went to Puerto Rico with five actors. Two played the GIs in *The Battle of Blood Island*, leaving the three in this film. Harold is played by Antony Carbone, who appeared in four Corman films and played the East Coast tough guy quite easily. Evelyn is played by the tall and striking-looking Betsy Jones-Moreland, another Corman regular. The third actor, playing Martin, was billed as Edward Wain. He was, in reality, Robert Towne, who wrote the script for this film, which explains the intelligence and the dark, doomed feel, and went on to become one of the greatest screenwriters of all time, winning an Academy Award for *Chinatown* (1974). Yes, Towne was yet another American film legend who got his start with Corman.

The Last Woman on Earth has yet another interesting back-story: typical of Corman's work, not only did Corman complete it and *Battle* on the Puerto Rico trip, but he went under budget and ahead of schedule. This left him with five extra days in Puerto Rico, unused footage, and enough money to make a *third* film—take that, Stanley Kubrick! That movie, *Creature from the Haunted Sea* (1961), also featured Carbone, Jones-Moreland, and Towne, but it was a goofy spy-monster farce featuring the inane narration, poor sound, and choppy editing reminiscent of *Little Shop of Horrors* (1960). It made money, of course, be-cause Corman made it for practically nothing and released it himself. Oh, and in that film—spoiler alert—Towne's character survives, while Carbone's and Jones-Moreland's get killed off. After Martin's sad finish in *The Last Woman on Earth*, I thought that was more than fair.

And here's an even better postscript to the Puerto Rican story: Corman considered making a *fourth* film on that trip. Wow.

17 and **18**

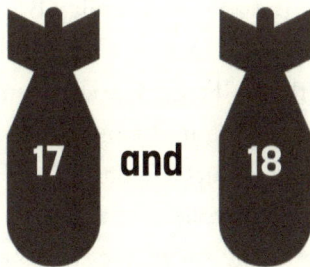

Las Vegas Hillbillys (1966) and Hillbillys in a Haunted House (1967): Not a Gamble for the Faint-Hearted

Believe it or not, there is a subgenre of bombs called *hillbilly movies*, and the films in it, usually comedies, range from the fairly good (*The Egg and I* [1949] and *No Time for Sergeants* [1958]) to the amusing (the "Ma and Pa Kettle" series), to the really awful. The last category includes movies like *Private Snuffy Smith* (1942) and anything starring Ferlin Husky.

Some well-meaning person—I think it was me—gave me a DVD collection of hillbilly movies, and all I can say is that I watched them so that you don't have to. Two in particular were particularly bad, and both featured Mr. Husky.

Some facts: the Missouri native was a founding father of the Grand Ole Opry and a multitalented country singer who could do ballads, honkytonk, rockabilly, folk, and many other country music styles and apparently had great stage presence. Husky's seven-decade career earned him a star on the Hollywood Walk of Fame for recording and induction into the Country Music

Hall of Fame. And, yes, Ferlin Husky was his real name, despite his best efforts. At the advice of Smiley Brunette, he recorded under other names such as Simon Crum and Terry Preston because he did not think "Ferlin Husky" would be accepted by audiences. He eventually found fame under his own name, recording a long string of hits such as "Gone" and "Wings of a Dove." But as that DVD collection attests, he was no actor.

A releasing company called the Woolner Brothers apparently let these movies escape in order to do for country music what the American International's *Beach Party* movies did for the California surf culture. That isn't setting your goal very high, yet they didn't really achieve it. Not that they didn't get a lot of help trying.

First, there is Mr. Husky. The Woolner Brothers obviously hoped to cash in on his rapport with audiences and his consistent popularity. But, alas, he is simply a terrible actor, delivering his lines in an unsure way while staring off into space, possibly looking at cue cards. He pauses, smiles, and stammers, leaving the viewer wondering if he was intoxicated during the filming. I have long suspected that some celebrities, forced into acting in bad movies in the '60s, got over their discomfort and lack of experience by arriving on the set smashed. I am thinking specifically of Dean Martin in all the Matt Helm movies.

Secondly, these movies hoped to lure in male viewers by featuring top-heavy bombshell blondes who sported gravity-defying bras and spouted sanity-defying inane dialogue. Thirdly, the films were mostly a showcase for top country-western acts at the time. Unfortunately, that move may have prevented broad audience appeal since the cornpone humor and Grand Ole Opry greats only appealed to the minority of people in the '60s who already liked country-western music and hillbilly films; this was five years before the first episode of *Hee-Haw*.

Las Vegas Hillbillys features Husky as an unassuming would-be country singer who makes money selling wood. His name is Woody—get it? He and his pal Jeepers, played by Opry comedian Don Bowman, drive out to Vegas to take over a casino left to Woody by a late uncle. They discover that the casino is actually a rundown, money-losing bar. There they meet the uncle's "protégé" (1966 for *mistress*), played as terribly as ever by Jayne Mansfield, and the uncle's "hire" (1966 for *mistress*), Boots Malone, played by Mamie van Doren. Apparently, in real life, the two actresses hated each other and refused to appear onscreen together; if you look closely, you'll see that the director used doubles for scenes where they are supposed to both be in the shot at the same time. That was probably not difficult since they were two of the infamous and lookalike three Ms of '50s–'60s movies: Mansfield, Mamie, and Monroe. Richard Kiel—see my review of *The Brute Man*—shows up as a henchman, there is a dancing motorcycle gang, and the thing actually ends—spoiler alert—with a pie fight.

The thin plot, terrible acting, and phony-looking sets—the kind with really high walls because they are obviously a studio—are just gimmicks to showcase endless country-western actors popular at the time, including "Whispering Bill" Anderson, Roy Drusky, Sonny James, Del Reeves, Opry comedian the Duke of Paducah, and the openly gay Wilma Burgess, who sings a gender-neutral song ("Sweet, Sweet Baby") so typical of her musical canon. The film has one great scene: a young Connie Smith takes the stage and, without even a pause, belts out "Nobody but a Fool." Her contralto voice and use of twangy background electric guitar set a precedent that defines country music to this day, and it's a great song.

Hillbillys in a Haunted House, which the Woolner Brothers released a year later, brings back Woody and Jeepers—why?—

for another wacky adventure. This time, Woody has become a successful country singer traveling to Nashville with Joi Lansing as Boots Malone, who replaces Ms. Van Doren without the audience really noticing; she is another bottle blonde with an unbelievable figure. Interestingly, in real life, Lansing, a '60s sex bomb who worked as a model, nightclub singer, and pinup, was actually a family-oriented, nonsmoking, teetotaling Mormon who never used drugs or posed nude. She did come close to the posing thing; Lansing released a video for the title song from *The Silencers* (1966; the first Matt Helm movie), in which she starts the song clothed in layers, but she peels them off during the number until she's down to a fairly teeny bikini. It's a terrible song, by the way.

This time, the nonsense involves our heroes, who are driving to Nashville for a "swingin' jamboree," being forced to spend the night in a haunted house for reasons too contrived to explain. Seems the place is not really haunted; all the spooky goings-on are being controlled by gadgets in the basement run by spies who are hiding out and using the contrived scares to drive away intruders. The spies have been hired to steal a rocket fuel formula from the nearby Acme City Rocket Plant. It's not disclosed who they work for, but their bosses all appear to be Chinese.

The three bad guys are played by former Universal horror-film stars Lon Chaney Jr., John Carradine, and Basil Rathbone. Apparently, the Woolner Brothers took another page out of the *Beach Party* book by casting these sad has-beens for audience appeal. It is depressing to hear these once-great actors reciting the terrible lines and stupid jokes, especially Rathbone, who tries his best by orating the pablum as if it were Shakespeare. This was actually the last film released while he was alive, bringing his great career to an embarrassing end. Even sadder is the fact that he followed this film with *Ghost in the Invisible Bikini*, released posthumously and a screen credit he shared with the equally great Francis X. Bushman; see my review of *Phantom Planet*.

Anyway, the goings-on involve a double agent, a gorilla, and a real ghost, and in the end—spoiler alert but no surprise—our heroes capture the spies, earn medals, and get to Nashville. The thin plot only takes up about forty-five of the eighty-five-minute running time. All the rest of the film is a showcase of more Grand Ole Opry stars performing for the camera, including Husky, Merle Haggard, Sonny James—who is surprisingly tall and, sadly, does *not* sing "Young Love"—and others who are largely lost to obscurity, except to diehard Opry fans. Oh, yeah, Bowman does a "funny song," which is neither sung nor funny, and Lansing does a few numbers. Like *The Silencers*, they are terrible songs, but she keeps her clothes on. Every time another star is performing, the camera cuts to Husky looking on. He is supposed to be looking like he is enjoying the songs and giving approval, but he has the expression of someone who is passing a kidney stone and trying not to moan.

I'm sure there are other hillbilly movies out there that I have not seen, but I will try to contain my viewer's curiosity.

19

Murder Is My Business (1946):
Ward Cleaver as a Tough-Guy Detective!

I love detective stories. I love to watch the detective move through the case, and I like to look for the slightest detail that may prove a valuable clue later on. For those not that familiar with whodunnits, here is a 100-level lesson: Detectives come in two general categories. First, there is the intellectual, or armchair, sleuth, typified by Sherlock Holmes, Hercules Poirot, Lord Peter Wimsey, and arguably Ellery Queen. Then there is the hard-boiled shamus, always getting knocked out and romancing the broads. This category includes Phillip Marlow, Sam Spade, and the toughest of them all, Mike Hammer, who frequently gets shot during cases while saving his beautiful secretary, Velma.

Prolific writer Rex Stout hit the literary jackpot when he came up with the idea of a team composed of one of each type of detective. Nero Wolfe, the rotund orchid-growing gourmet, was the armchair-anchored brains, while Archie Goodwin was his brave and energetic leg man. Archie, often at personal risk and usually with some romancing of the women he meets, assembled the clues and brought them to Wolfe, who then solved the crimes.

In the hardboiled category, one of the busiest and most popular detectives was Michael Shayne, the creation of Brett Halliday, a pseudonym for Davis Dresser. The prolific Dresser wrote fifty Shayne novels, but that was only the beginning of the Shayne franchise, which expanded to ghostwritten stories, a monthly magazine, a long-running radio show, a TV show, and twelve movies. The recurring characters in Dresser's stories included Shayne, reporter Tim Rourke, policeman Lt. Gentry, and Shayne's secretary, Lucy Hamilton. Initially Shayne is married to a woman named Phyllis, but she gets killed off relatively early in the books, which switched the mood of the series from comic to dark and more brooding.

The first seven of the twelve films were produced by 20th Century Fox, starred Lloyd Nolan, and were relatively high-budget compared to the five that followed, made by Producers Releasing Corporation (PRC) and starring Ward Cleaver—I mean, Hugh Beaumont. PRC was a Poverty Row studio that churned out 179 low-budget films from 1939 to 1947, never spending more than $100,000 on a single film. Their Shayne films were strictly assembly-line B pictures, shot with frequent use of rear-screen projection and reused studio sets and props. PRC certainly could not afford a star like Nolan, so they turned to Beaumont, a Kansas-born lay Methodist minister who had graduated from USC with a degree in Theology and who was a commanding officer during WWII but served as a chaplain. He made dozens of uncredited film appearances, had a somewhat notable turn as Alan Ladd's friend in *The Blue Dahlia* (1946), and had starred with child star Jerry Mathers in a short religious film, which led to his being cast as Ward Cleaver. On screen and off, Beaumont was a nice, gentle fellow. So how did he pull off playing tough guy Michael Shayne? Basically, by talking tough, eating a lot of peanuts in the shell, and cracking jokes and smiling at everyone.

Murder Is My Business (1946) is the first of the five Shayne-PRC films and features a typical plot that sets up a murder and five potential suspects. Based on *The Uncomplaining Corpses*, which Halliday had written five years before, the story involves a wealthy but stingy woman who is found strangled. The suspects include her allowance-restricted husband, who now stands to get everything; her ex-con brother; her rather foolish stepson; her spoiled stepdaughter; and the stepdaughter's gigolo boyfriend. The one person the audience doesn't suspect is the person the dimwitted police detective thinks did it, Shayne's friend Joe Darnell, who was in the wrong place at the wrong time and was shot dead over the strangled woman's body by the husband. Joe's wife blames Shayne and tries to shoot him but is thwarted by Tim Rourke. With me so far?

Anyway, nearly getting killed by Ms. Darnell convinces Shayne to solve the crime and give her the $1,000 he collects. What a guy. Helping Shayne are his friend Tim and his secretary, Phyllis, apparently not his wife yet, who is played by Cheryl Walker. Ms. Walker was a model who had a brief film career but retired early to lead anticommunist efforts in the 1950s. One running gag is that Shayne is constantly getting knocked out by the loutish ex-con brother, played by the ubiquitous Lyle Talbot; see my reviews for *The Thirteenth Guest* and *Jail Bait*. Like other films of this type, the action hurries along to cram the story into the short, sixty-three-minute running time, leaving lots of peanut shells and leading up to—spoiler alert—a rather obvious conclusion.

Murder Is My Business, which rips off its title from *Trouble Is My Business*, an excellent collection of Phillip Marlowe stories, is no *Murder on the Orient Express*, but it is a pleasant diversion, and it's fun to see Beaver's dad as a tough private detective. I think I'll check out the other four films. Maybe Ken Osmond, who played Eddie Haskell in *Leave It to Beaver*, will turn up in the role of a bad guy, and Mr. Cleaver will finally get a chance to shoot him.

20

Michael Shayne, Private Detective (1940): A Better Bomb?

As I mentioned in the previous review, when Producers Releasing Corporation (PRC) Studios acquired the Michael Shayne franchise from 20th Century Fox, the films naturally went low-budget. That made me wonder: were the 20th Century Fox films really "better bombs"? Naturally, I decided to answer that question by looking at those films. To paraphrase Julie Andrews, I started at the very beginning, a very good place to start.

And so I started with *Michael Shayne, Private Detective*, the first of the Fox films, made in 1940. That may not be a fair comparison since that film was made six years earlier than *Murder Is My Business* (1946; see prior review). Nonetheless, the older film is clearly the better technically: the rear-screen projection and use of stock footage are better, there are views out the windows of the sets, the sets are larger and more lavish, and the writing is better.

The casting is better too; not only does Lloyd Nolan play Shayne, but he is supported by a cadre of Fox regulars. Marjorie

Weaver plays annoying rich girl turned heroine, Phyllis Brighton. A perky brunette, Fox placed Weaver in twenty-seven B pictures; she hit her career zenith in 1939 playing opposite Henry Fonda in *Young Mister Lincoln*. The "bad girl" is played by Joan Valerie, who had a similar B-picture career as Weaver; Fox cast them both in the lucrative Charlie Chan films. Walter Abel's face is familiar to old movie fans from his more than sixty films, including such diverse movies as *The Three Musketeers* (1935) and *Holiday Inn* (1942). Here he plays a mousy gambler who actually turns out to be a fairly key character. Ubiquitous character actress Elizabeth Patterson, who later popped up—popped out?—in *I Love Lucy* as next-door neighbor Ms. Trumbull, provides comic relief as an amateur detective helping Shayne, and Donald McBride, a veteran of 140 B pictures, provides more comedy as the befuddled police chief who Shayne outsmarts at every turn, a staple in such movies. The film features other Fox employees Douglass Dumbrille, Charles Kolb, and George Meeker, but the most pleasant surprise in the cast is Charles Coleman as Patterson's butler, Ponsby. I always associate Coleman, a veteran of innumerable films, with the more vocal and larger of the two businessmen who try to get Reginald Owen's Scrooge to donate to the poor "to buy some meat and drink" in the 1938 version of *A Christmas Carol*. He's the guy who asks Mr. Scrooge if he is "in earnest" about that mysterious offer Scrooge whispers into his ear. Maybe Scrooge was offering him a Michael Shayne seven-picture deal with Fox.

At 77 minutes, the running time is still short compared to A-quality detective films like *The Maltese Falcon*, made a year later at 101 minutes, but it's longer than most B detective films. Even that is not enough time to tell the convoluted story, so that much of the plot happens offscreen. Shayne is hired to watch after spoiled rich girl Phyllis—future wife, maybe?—played by

Weaver, who is getting into trouble by gambling and dating bad boy Meeker. To scare Phyllis off of her boyfriend, Shayne knocks him out, puts him in a car, puts ketchup on him to pretend he has been shot, and then shows him to Phyllis to convince her that he is dead and that's what happens to bad boys. But—surprise—they find that he really has been shot dead and apparently with Shayne's gun. The rest of the movie is spent, naturally, with Shayne trying to clear his name by solving the murder. The solution involves horserace doping, blackmail, switched gun barrels, and women's clothes. It's all so complicated that I couldn't provide a spoiler alert if I wanted to. Just know that Nolan's Shayne grinned his way through six more such films with Fox, and then, well, you know the rest of the story.

All in all, *Michael Shayne, Private Detective* is not that different from *Murder Is My Business*: They are both short, breezy, complicated, played for laughs, and eminently forgettable, although the former clearly had better production values and a little more coin behind it. Both are fun to watch. And, coincidentally, both feature actors who acted tough and shady onscreen but were fairly clean-cut in real life: Beaumont was a Methodist minister, and Nolan, the son of Irish immigrants, was a lifelong Christian who lobbied unsuccessfully to get prayer into public school; stayed married to his first wife, Mell, for forty-eight years until her death in 1981; established a foundation for autism; and got the Reagan administration to pass legislation requiring education for autistic children. Not bad for a gumshoe who called all women *toots*.

21

Time to Kill (1942): Passing the Bomb

By 1942, 20th Century Fox had made six Michael Shayne movies in three years, and the studio decided it was time to pass the baton—or pass the bomb, if you prefer—to another studio. And pass it they did. Fox sold the franchise to Poverty Row studio PRC; see my review of *Murder Is My Business*. When one looks at the seventh and last Shayne film they made, 1942's *Time to Kill*, the viewer sees a portrait of the studio losing interest.

First, there is the running time; coming in at fifty-nine minutes, the film is not even an hour long, and about ten minutes of *that* is used up listening to a torch singer belt out some forgettable tunes. Secondly, there's the story; it's not even a Michael Shayne story, and it has nothing to do with the writings of Brett Halliday. Rather, 1942 seemed to be a tough year for Raymond Chandler and his most famous—and my second favorite—detective, Phillip Marlowe. That year, Chandler sold his first two Marlowe stories to Hollywood, but in neither was Marlowe allowed to appear. The first story, *Farewell My Lovely*, became RKO's *The Falcon Takes Over*. In that film, the Falcon, played as always by George Sanders, takes over the Marlowe role, and the great story debuted as just another Falcon serialized romp. The second Chandler story, *The High Window*, became *Time to Kill*, with Nolan's Shayne taking the Marlowe role.

It wasn't until 1944's *Murder My Sweet* that movie audiences learned Marlowe's name. In that film, RKO again used the *Farewell My Lovely* story, this time casting Alan Ladd as Marlowe and sticking closer to the book and the character. That film is credited as being one of the first films noir and raised audiences' interest in Marlowe, which was cemented when he was played two years later by Humphrey Bogart in the amazing *The Big Sleep*, a movie so wonderfully complicated that I once went to a rerun movie house and watched it three times in a row to make sure I caught all the dialogue and intricacies of the plot.

For the record, *The High Window* was filmed again in 1947, this time with George Montgomery playing Marlowe and 20th Century Fox spending some coin on a seventy-two-minute running time and an A-list cast. Fox released that film as *The High Window* in the United Kingdom but called it *The Brasher Doubloon* in the United States. The film is more faithful to the book and the character, and the US title is not as weird as it sounds. The story involves Marlowe getting hired by a wealthy widow to find an extremely valuable old US coin, a brasher doubloon, which she believes was stolen by her son's torch singer wife. She asks Marlowe to both find the coin and persuade the wife to leave the son and town. The coin was left to the widow by her husband, who fell to his death, apparently accidentally, from the titular high window a few years before.

The assignment seems routine enough, but soon Marlowe discovers that the son is a lout, the torch singer is OK, and the theft of the coin was part of a complex forgery racket that is leading to murders. *The Brasher Doubloon*, which was filmed as a noir, better captured the typical dark Chandler elements and the tired, good-guy Marlowe persona than *Time to Kill* did, as our hero—spoiler alert—rescues the wealthy widow's timid and neurotic secretary from blackmail and danger.

Time to Kill instead reduces the very good *Doubloon* story to a fortysomething-minute cheaply made film that trades comedy for plot. Most of that story is actually told by Shayne to the cast, and therefore the audience, to save screen time and production. Filmed on standard sets, the film's cast includes second-string character actors such as Heather Angel, who later found some fame in cartoon voice work; Doris Merrick; Ralph Byrd, who himself found work as a movie detective in serial films, playing Dick Tracy; Richard Lane; and Sheila Bromley. Yes, 20th Century saw Phillip Marlowe's star rising, as *The Brasher Doubloon* attests, but they put Michael Shayne on the movie auction block, and he apparently went cheap to PRC.

But don't feel bad for Mike Shayne. Although his film career ended in 1946 with the last PRC cheapie, *Too Many Winners*, Shayne lived on in an excellent weekly radio show starring Jeff Chandler and Wally Maher (1944–1953), some comic books, a thirty-two-episode TV show featuring Richard Denning (1960), and his own mystery magazine, which was published for nearly thirty years. Knowing how writers like to reuse stories and characters—see my review of *Dark Mountain*—I'm sure the future holds more Mike. Shayne was one of the original hardboiled good-guy detectives, and despite some mediocre—at best—serial films, it will be hard to keep a successful character down.

22

Goodbye Charlie (1964): The A-List Movie as a Bomb

B pictures are an obvious source of bombs, but can an A-list picture be a bomb? Absolutely. Cinema history is full of A films that bombed, are bombs, or both. Remember, I define *bombs* as movies that are enjoyable in their terribleness and/or weirdness and are often forgotten. They are often cheaply made, filmed in black and white, and "star" folks you never heard of. But there are exceptions to these other features; some bombs were expensive or even handsomely made, in color, and with big-name casts. Yet as films, they are just *awful*.

A great example is *Goodbye Charlie*, a film I actually saw a while ago but forgot that I had seen until I recently heard one of its stars, Pat Boone, talking about it on a radio show. I went back and looked at it again and realized the reason for my amnesia; it is cringingly bad. Yet this film was directed by Vincent Minelli and based on a play by George Axelrod.

The film begins with a scene later repeated in *Boogie Nights* (1997); a man walks into a crazy party filled with all kinds of people and noise, proceeds into a bedroom, sees his wife in bed with another man, and shoots the guy dead. In the case of

Goodbye Charlie, the shooter is Walter Matthau, playing a Greek movie mogul; the party setting is his yacht; and the man he shoots is the titular Charlie, an actor and ladies' man who tries to escape through a porthole and literally makes a splash in front of all the partygoers.

Cut to a cute animated Rankin-Bass-type opening in which we watch a cartoon Charlie sink to the bottom of the ocean while animated sea creatures swim by and Pat Boone and a 1960s chorus sing the title song, written, by the way, by Andre Previn. Yes, the studio spent money on this film. The lyrics make fun of Charlie's demise. The film then continues by introducing Charlie's best friend, George, played by Tony Curtis—more expense—a screenwriter from Paris who has flown in to give his buddy's eulogy at Charlie's Malibu beach house. The eulogy is sparsely attended, given Charlie's user personality: just George, Charlie's agent, and two old flames—one played by a young Ellen Burstyn, who is introduced as the wife of a producer named Saltzman. I don't know if that was a direct nod to Harry Saltzman, the producer of the first James Bond films. Anyway, George makes a sad speech, bids the two women goodbye, and then meets with the agent, learning that he is the executor of Charlie's "estate"—all debts. The agent leaves, and George pours himself a drink and slumps into a chair.

The doorbell rings, and enter Debbie Reynolds and Pat Boone. Boone plays an outrageously rich young man who found Reynolds wet, naked, and wandering on the beach road. She is wearing his oversized raincoat that he hastily threw on her, and there are a lot of silly innuendos about these facts. Reynold's character has that old '60s movie gimmick of amnesia, and George tries to take her to a hospital, but she refuses, so he puts her to bed. George sleeps on the couch, of course; this is a sanitized '60s sex farce like just about any film made at the same time starring Doris Day paired with Rock Hudson or James Garner.

Then it gets really weird. Debbie's character wakes up the next day screaming; she has realized that she is the reincarnation of Charlie. She/he convinces George of this fact by recounting stuff only Charlie would know and does an embarrassing stretch of acting by trying to come across as a macho ladies' man. What follows is some gender-bending strangeness wherein Charlie shows George his/her breasts—off camera, of course—discovers his/her feminine wiles, and uses them to seduce Pat Boone and extort money from the two women who attended his/her eulogy. Eventually, Charlie feels remorse and makes things right, but no matter; Charlie (male) gets his comeuppance when the Walter Matthau character tries to seduce Charlie (female), and Charlie (female)—spoiler alert—is once again shot, this time by Matthau's wife. Charlie (female) falls back into the sea, now killed twice—by both the jealous husband and his jealous wife. The irony is the point of the movie, and the viewer gets it. However, despite—another spoiler alert—the tacked-on "happy" ending, the movie leaves you with that "OK . . . so?" feeling.

Even in these days of apparently over a hundred genders, gender-affirming surgery, and same-sex relationships, the film is weird and unpleasant. The producers were obviously trying to repeat the success of *Some Like It Hot* (1959), which also starred Curtis, but they failed. *Goodbye Charlie* lost money in 1964 and is the kind of bomb you want to forget about today. Too bad the producers did not take a hint from the fact that the Axelrod play it's based on closed after a limited run, despite the casting of Lauren Bacall as Charlie.

The acting in *Goodbye Charlie* is pretty bad, a reminder that even an A-list cast cannot shine you-know-what. Conversely, even a B-list cast can do OK with better material; see my review of *The Last Woman on Earth*. And this cast was given *much* better material in other films. In 1959 and 1960, Tony Curtis was amazing in *The Defiant Ones* and *Spartacus*, respectively, roles that earned him Golden Globe and Academy Award nominations. Sadly, *Goodbye Charlie* was a turning point in his career; starting with this film, he landed roles mostly in silly comedies and sex farces. The exception to this downward trend was his underrated turn as the titular character in *The Boston Strangler* (1968), a film marred by the use of the then-fad of collage editing.

Similarly, no matter how one feels about the now non-PC *How the West Was Won* (1962), it can be agreed that Debbie Reynolds was a standout in that film. In 1964, she hit another high point with her titular role in *The Unsinkable Molly Brown* before sinking back into stupid sex comedies like 1968's *How Sweet It Is*, in which she starred with James Garner, of course. As for Walter Matthau, he was able to find his way out of career hell despite this bomb: 1964 also saw him in *Fail Safe*; 1965 brought the wonderful *Mirage* as Ted Casell, the eager but doomed newly minted private detective; and in 1966, he won his Academy Award for playing Oscar Madison in *The Odd Couple*.

Interestingly, there is a cinema legend that says Pat Boone was inebriated during his scenes. As I have mentioned in other reviews, I have a weird interest in actors who get through their recitation of bad material, or make the film a bomb, by showing up on the set smashed. Although Boone did have a scene in *Goodbye Charlie* where he pretends to be drunk, I didn't see evidence that he actually was. Write to me if you know otherwise. He certainly didn't mention it on that radio show.

Regardless, the point is clear: A-list films can be bombs *and* bomb at the box office. *Goodbye Charlie* is proof of both.

23

The Horror of Party Beach (1964): Chocolate Sauce and Gutzon Borglum

Here's a trivia question: what do two of the best movies ever made have in common with one of the worst? Answer: chocolate sauce and Gutzon Borglum. More on that later.

Recently, I read a magazine article that was a loving tribute to drive-in movies. The article listed several films as typical examples of "good" drive-in fare. The author hit the mark on most but made the mistake of listing *The Horror of Party Beach*. The author correctly noted that the makers of this film figured that since teen drive-in goers liked beach movies and monster movies, they decided to combine the genres. The author forgot to mention that the result was a bomb that makes just about everyone's list of the worst movies of all time. Ignoring that fact, I decided to follow the author's apparent affection for the film, which they called "fun viewing," and take a peek. All I can say is that I watched it so that you don't have to.

Z-grade filmmaker Del Tenney didn't even leave his home state of Connecticut to film this thing; yes, *Party Beach* is in the Nutmeg, not the Golden, State. The movie features local Connecticut actors, a local Connecticut motorcycle gang—I guess they had one—and a Connecticut rock band, the Del Aires, who were apparently quite popular in Connecticut at the time. So it is basically a regional film; see my review of *The Yesterday Machine*. As the action shifts from Party Beach to a formal dance to an outdoor concert, the Del Aires seem to be the only band around. They sing all six of their "hits" in the course of the movie, but thanks to the terrible audio quality and editing, they all sound the same—and maybe they just weren't good songs.

The insipid story opens with two guys on a boat dropping barrels labeled "Danger: Radioactive Waste" into the ocean off Party Beach. The barrels sink to the bottom and open, dousing their contents onto skeletons of people who apparently died in shipwrecks. What follows is a long, boring FX scene in which one of the skulls slowly morphs into a gill-face similar to the one in *The Creature from the Black Lagoon* (1954), only more plastic-looking and with its mouth stuffed full of things that look like bratwurst. The scene was shot through a fish tank, so we see goldfish swimming around during the entire sequence.

Back on Party Beach, the assistant to a Famous Scientist is arguing with his cute but drunk girlfriend. Her shenanigans get him into a fight with the leader of the motorcycle gang. The two men fight in a kind of a dance that looks exactly like a choreographed scene from *West Side Story*, similar to the antics in *Phantom Planet*; see my review. They shake hands in the end, but all is not well; the drunken girlfriend has swum off, right into the clutches of Gill-Face, who claws her to death, covering her body with chocolate sauce. I could tell it was chocolate sauce because the version I saw had been colorized. The colorization technique, by the way, was the worst I have ever seen. The color kept shifting from green to blue to yellow tint, making it look like the filmmakers had used one of those plastic color disks that were rotated in front of light bulbs to change the color of Christmas displays in the '60s.

The assistant to the Famous Scientist is obviously distressed to see his girlfriend wash up on the beach covered with chocolate sauce, but he recovers quickly thanks to the fact that he is really in love with the daughter of the Famous Scientist. Tall and blond, you can tell she is a good girl because she wears long dresses and sensible shoes.

Meanwhile, Gill-Face and his friends—there are apparently more than one—crash a slumber party attended by dozens of girls dressed in identical long white nightgowns and singing folk songs. The women let the monsters in because they think they are frat boys. They even put a bucket of water above the door. Needless to say, the water does not stop the gill-faces, and much screaming and chocolate sauce result. A radio tells us that twenty more girls were killed. The giant snails in *The Monster That Challenged the World*, who only killed a few people, can't hold a candle to these creatures.

After a few more women get killed, this time due to a flat tire and bad directions, the Famous Scientist gets involved, spouting some of the worst movie pseudo-science I have ever heard, even worse than the aforementioned drivel in *The Yesterday Machine*—nonsense about amoebas and the living dead. He finally discovers that they can be killed by "plain, good old" sodium chloride. Two drunken men are killed next, apparently to show that the monsters aren't misogynists, which is too bad because they were the best actors in the picture. There is actually a scene where the assistant to the Famous Scientist, unable to find sodium chloride (i.e., table salt) anywhere in Connecticut, drives to New York City to get it from someplace labeled with a big sign that says *New York Chemical Company.*

Meanwhile, the daughter of the Famous Scientist bumps into the gill-faces, who come at her in the slowest monster attack ever, giving the Famous Scientist, the police, and the assistant to the Famous Scientist, who is driving all the way back from NYC, enough time to come to her rescue. The whole thing ends—spoiler alert but not really—with a fight involving sodium chloride and monsters bursting into flames. For creatures born in the ocean, they sure are salt-sensitive.

There are no notable actors in the cast, with the possible exception of Eulabelle Moore. Moore was actually a fairly respectable Broadway actress, but, sadly, this was her last role; she died shortly after this stinker was released. Hers is a cringingly terrible part, a stereotypical Black maid for the Famous Scientist named—wait for it—Eulabelle. The Famous Scientist either scolds or mocks Eulabelle for her silly rants about voodoo and black magic. Yet she is actually the one who discovers that the monsters are killed by sodium chloride and that there is sodium chloride at the New York Chemical Company, but does she get credit? Of course not—it's 1964.

So back to the trivia question. As readers of these reviews know, I am a huge admirer of Hitchcock, and two of his finest works from 1959 and 1960 were *North by Northwest* and *Psycho,* respectively. In the later film, Hitchcock used chocolate sauce for blood—that's probably where Del Tenney got the idea—but got away with it because his film was in black and white. The former film famously featured a chase down Mount Rushmore, carved by prolific American sculptor Gutzon Borglum. Although Borglum died in 1941, he left behind a studio and sculpting company based in Connecticut. By 1964, the studio must have really needed money; the gill-face masks were created there.

Too bad. Borglum left impressive works all across the United States. However, he was a Freemason and a Klan sympathizer; it probably won't be long before all his work is torn down or sandblasted away. I am surprised that the statue he created in my hometown of Portland, Oregon, hasn't yet been toppled by the local riot mob; it is a larger-than-life figure of the *Oregonian* newspaper founder Harvey Scott, which stands on the top of Portland's Mount Tabor. Nearby the statue *was* a bust of York, of Lewis and Clark fame, which was defaced and toppled by rioters because, apparently, statues honoring the first African native to cast a vote in North America are racist.

Anyway, the statue of Scott is infamous in Portland; Borglum sculpted Scott with his arm raised and a scowl on his face. He looks, well, really pissed, like someone who actually paid to see *The Horror of Party Beach* and wants their money back.

24

High School Big Shot (1959):
Old Teenagers, Cheap Sets, and James Dean

Here's that trivia question again: what do two of the best movies ever made have in common with one of the worst? Answer this time: Malcolm Atterbury, Stanley Adams, and a faulty suitcase. More on those, well, now.

In 1956, Stanley Kubrick made his first of many masterpieces, a tight and tough crime drama called *The Killing*. The story involves a high-yield robbery, a double cross, a shocking scene where the crossed and double-crossed have a sudden shootout, and a downbeat ending—spoiler alert—where the money is lost thanks to a faulty suitcase. If you have never seen *The Killing*, you are in for a treat; the film displays early Kubrick touches, including a long tracking shot of the previously mentioned shootout through multiple rooms using a 25mm wide-angle lens to cause image distortion.

Three years later, the plot of *The Killing* was ripped off in a low-budget cheapie called *High School Big Shot*. Although the film gives no credit to the source novel, *Clean Break* by Lionel

White, or the original screenwriter who adapted it, the great hardboiled crime writer Jim Thompson, writer and director Joel Rapp—see my review of *The Battle of Blood Island* (1960)—obviously used the basic story from Kubrick's film. Kubrick, who by 1959 was filming *Spartacus*, obviously had other things to do than come after the makers of this bomb, who included Roger Corman and Filmgroup. Corman, of course, often "borrowed" from any available source.

The twist in this version of the story is told in the title: high school whiz kid Marv Grant plots to steal $1 million from the shipping office where he works after school. Marv enlists the help of a noted safecracker, Harry March, and his brother-in-law, Sam. Marv wants to help his deadbeat alcoholic father and impress his girlfriend, Betty, who in reality is only using him to write her term paper for English class. Betty entices her loutish boyfriend, Vince, to follow Marv and his accomplices and then steal the money from them. Once again—spoiler alert—there is a sudden shootout, a downbeat ending, and the money is lost thanks to a faulty suitcase.

Unlike *The Killing*, which cost—and lost—Kubrick plenty, including the salary of the great cinematographer Lucien Ballard, *High School Big Shot*, like all Filmgroup productions, was a serious cheapie. It was filmed almost entirely on five cheap-looking sets, including a classroom, a high school exit door, Marv's apartment, a liquor store, and the shipping office. Those and some external shots on a LA wharf make up the entire production design.

I'll say this for *High School Big Shot*: unlike *The Horror of Party Beach*, which had *no* recognizable actors, the film has a lot of familiar faces. It utilized some remarkably familiar character actors whom you have seen innumerable times but never knew their names. Peter Leeds, who made nearly eight thousand movie and TV show appearances, is Marv's English teacher. To answer the other part of the trivia question, two other familiar faces, Malcolm Atterbury and Stanley Adams, appear as Marv's drunken father and safecracker Harry March, respectively. Both men also appeared in one of the best, and my favorite, films ever, Hitchcock's *North by Northwest*, released the same year (1959). In that film, Adams appears as a detective, and Atterbury is the farmer at Prairie Stop who utters the famous line about the plane dusting crops where there "ain't no crops."

The most interesting person in the cast, Tom Pittman, was a tragic figure whose life mirrored that of James Dean. Like Dean, he was a promising actor who appeared in a few films before his sudden death. Also like Dean, he was celebrated posthumously. Weirdly, both he and Dean died in car accidents while they were driving Porsche Spyders. While Dean's three films (*Giant* [1956], *East of Eden* [1955], and *Rebel Without a Cause* [1955]) obviously topped Pittman's twelve smaller roles in TV and bombs—his role as Marv in *High School Big Shot* was his last and largest role—Pittman's car crash was more spectacular than Dean's. Dean simply piled into a sedan that was turning left in front of him, while Pittman went over a guardrail and plunged down a 150-foot ravine. Unwitnessed, the crash was not discovered for twenty days until the police searched Pittman's known driving routes.

I can't resist more comparisons: both Dean and Pittman played teenagers in their last films, which were released posthumously. Both were in their midtwenties—Pittman was twenty-six, and Dean was twenty-four—and they certainly didn't look like teenagers in those movies. At least Dean looked youthful; in *Giant*, he dyed his hair gray and shaved some of it to make it look like he had a receding hairline for some of the later scenes. Conversely, the "teenagers" in *High School Big Shot* are some of the oldest teens you'll see in the movies. In contrast to Dean's boyish good looks, Pittman had coarse features and big lips. When the film was lampooned in the sixth season of *MST3000*, Mike Nelson and his robot friends mercilessly made fun of Pittman's looks and his character's mousy demeanor.

Despite the downbeat story and the cheap production values, I actually recommend that you take a look at *High School Big Shot*. It is only sixty-one minutes long, entertaining in the way a bomb is, and makes particularly interesting viewing when seen alongside *The Killing*. You might actually like Rapp and Corman's version of the story better, but I doubt it.

25

I Accuse My Parents (1944):
Pack Your Bags, Folks, You're Going on a Guilt Trip

In the mid-twentieth century, there was a genre of bombs I call *morality films*—movies that attempted to teach morals to various audiences. These target audiences included teenagers (e.g., *Reefer Madness* [1936]), society at large (e.g., *The Boy with Green Hair* [1948]), and, occasionally, parents. A good—bad?—example of the third kind is *I Accuse My Parents*.

I Accuse My Parents has a fairly typical plot: wealthy parents give their kid money but no affection, so that kid goes to work for the mob and commits manslaughter. Just kidding. This is an exploitation film, and like all such films, it is extreme, preachy, and fairly unbelievable.

The movie begins at the end, which is itself the ultimate spoiler. Teenager Jimmy is on trial for manslaughter. Found guilty, Jimmy is asked by the judge if he has anything to say before sentence is passed, whereupon Jimmy utters the titular phrase. Seems Jimmy's delinquency is all his parents' fault. The story then goes into flashback to show where Jimmy's parents went wrong. The movie shows them as a rich, dysfunctional couple that gives Jimmy everything but love. An only child, Jimmy has to cover up his mom's alcoholism and ignore his dad's philandering. Instead of spending time with his son, Dad just gives him money to "have a good time."

The last straw for Jimmy comes when he wins an essay contest at school by writing about how idyllic his home life is—yes, he includes a sentence about how a mother's job is to stay at home to make it a happy one. The judges invite his wonderful-sounding mom to the graduation planning committee, but she shows up drunk. Then his parents go off with their respective friends to party for the weekend, leaving Jimmy to celebrate his birthday alone.

Feeling lonely and neglected, Jimmy seeks solace, and then love, from Kitty, a woman he meets in a shoe store. But, alas, torch singer Kitty is the moll of gangster Charlie Blake, who entices Jimmy to run "errands" for him. Jimmy doesn't learn the real nature of these errands until he finds himself driving a getaway car for two bank robbers who have just killed a guard. Determined to spill the beans to the police, Jimmy is nearly rubbed out on Charlie's orders but escapes to a small town, where he is befriended by Al, a diner owner and reformed criminal. Al invites Jimmy to live with him as long as they go to church together on Sunday. Yeah, it's a really old film.

Jimmy still wants to turn Charlie in, so Al agrees to take him home and to the police. Things go wrong, and Jimmy ends up shooting and killing Charlie. Back in the courtroom, with Al, Kitty, and Jimmy's parents all present, the judge decides that the evidence supports Jimmy's story and releases him to the custody of his parents, who, the judge warns them, had better shape up. He then looks at the camera and says he hopes that the story helps *all* parents out there.

Ugh. As the saying goes, you reach an age where you have to stop blaming your parents. This blame-the-parents-for-juvenile-delinquency story will have none of that but actually fits in well with the current shame and blame attitude in the United States.

Besides being silly and simplistic, *I Accuse My Parents* is a serious bomb made on cheap sets by the Poverty Row studio Producers Releasing Corporation (PRC; see my review of *Murder Is My Business*) with a cast of B-picture character actors who each made hundreds of such films, including the ubiquitous George Meeker. Meeker appeared in so many movies—see, again, my review of *Murder Is My Business* and *Michael Shayne, Private Detective*—that he actually appeared in a few good ones, including *Gone with the Wind* (1939) and *Casablanca* (1942), and has a star on the Hollywood Walk of Fame, probably awarded for sheer effort. The cast also includes B-picture stars Mary Beth Hughes (Kitty) and George Lloyd. Lloyd will look familiar to you from Three Stooges shorts, and Hughes, who was probably not a singer, lip syncs three long and forgettable ballads. If you fast forward through them, you can watch the film in only fifty minutes!

Lampooned mercilessly in the fifth season of *MST3000*, *I Accuse My Parents* is not great cinema, but it is a good example of (1) the kind of cautionary exploitation tales rammed at audiences in the '30s, '40s, and '50s and (2) films that were rediscovered in the '70s and '80s by dope-smoking audiences who howled in laughter at them in rerun movie houses. I don't know; I think these movies have a kind of sweet innocence that is long gone, although many would say good riddance.

26

The Flight That Disappeared (1961): A Bomb about the Bomb

A subgenre of morality films popular in the '50s and '60s was the antinuke film, warning audiences of what John F. Kennedy called the "nuclear sword of Damocles"—the looming and constant threat of nuclear war. The genre hit the big screen in 1951, just six years after H-bombs were dropped on Japan, with the classic *The Day the Earth Stood Still* and reached a zenith in 1964 with the release of both *Fail Safe* and *Dr. Strangelove*. These two films basically put an end to the Strategic Air Command. Along the way, the genre included a weird little film released by United Artists in 1961 called *The Flight That Disappeared*. If this film had been made a few years later, it would have been a made-for-TV movie; it has low production values, comes in at just seventy-two minutes, stars character actors from TV you've never heard of, and was clearly made on the cheap.

I saw this film a few years ago and watched it again recently. It does not improve on repeated viewing; the fact that I have seen it twice is worth a t-shirt. As I have said, one of my definitions of *bombs* is that they are often forgotten movies, and this film, like the titular flight, has also largely disappeared from the public's memory, save for the rare viewing in obscure time slots on Turner Classic Movies. That said, I do wonder if the writers who dreamed up the recent TV series *Manifest* used this as source material but would not admit it under pain of death. Both stories involve disappearing aircraft—one for twenty-four hours, one for five and a half years—with occupants returning with otherworldly knowledge that ends up doing good.

The movie opens with passengers boarding a DC-6 at Los Angeles International Airport before the modern LAX appeared in the late '60s and has subsequently been remodeled / added on to about ten thousand times. You get to see footage of the old airport, people boarding from the tarmac, and interiors of the DC-6, another great aircraft that was actually built to compete with the Stratocruiser; see my review of *Home to Danger*. Both aircrafts were built for WWII but retooled for passenger flight, and both were prop planes despite the fact that the movie poster calls the plane a "jet airliner."

On board are three scientists—Tom Endicott, a rocket engineer; Marcia Paxton, a mathematician; and Dr. Carl Morris—en route to a meeting in Washington, DC, to begin planning construction of a "beta bomb" and a rocket to carry it. I guess a "B-bomb" is one bomb more powerful than an A-bomb. *Doctor* Morris is apparently the only one of the three scientists with a doctorate: the other two call him "Doctor," he informs the flight attendant that he is *Doctor* Morris, and he has a goatee, so he must be a doctor.

There is a lot of what I call *cinematic convenience* in the film; every time our three heroes need to have an important conversation, they go into the lounge in the back of the plane, and it happens to be empty except for them. They also happen to be the first people off the plane, so they can overhear the captain being told about the twenty-four-hour delay. Cinematic convenience always puts an empty parking space in front of where the character is going, even if it's supposed to be in New York City (e.g., the New York Chemical Company scene in *The Horror of Party Beach*).

The plane takes off, and all is well until it starts to climb uncontrollably, leading to a loss of oxygen. This was before drop-down oxygen masks. There is only one tank of O2 on the plane, and the flight attendants—let's face it: they were called *stewardesses* then—run around giving whiffs to people as they pass out one by one. This leads to my favorite bit of dialogue in the film: Endicott, who is seated next to Marcia, starts hitting on her while they both smoke away (it's 1961). She informs him that her cigarettes won't stay lit, whereupon Endicott tells her it's due to the lack of oxygen. Marcia smiles and tells him that's OK because the "no smoking" sign has just come on. Endicott is the last one to pass out and witnesses a crazed passenger jump out of the plane just before he does.

The plane parks on a cloud—no, Mick Jagger is not around—that has rocks and lots of dry-ice smoke and people walking around in nice Munsingwear casual shirts and matching black pants. Only the three scientists wake up, go out on the cloud, and discover that these people are from the future and have gathered to judge the scientists because the beta bomb destroyed Earth. The spokesperson of the Munsingwear people shows the scientists pictures of the destroyed planet, which is stock footage from Hiroshima. Poor Doctor Morris sputters in shame and surprise at the news; he thought the beta bomb would only be used for peaceful purposes. Apparently, the guy was not that smart after all, despite his doctorate and goatee.

The scientists are found guilty, of course, and their punishment is to stay on the cloud forever. After they hear the verdict, Endicott basically says "screw you" to the spokesperson and suggests to the others that they run for the plane and fly away. Alas, the plane is gone! Just as it looks like our three friends really are doomed to stay on the cloud for eternity, an older, even wiser-looking spokesperson, also in a Munsingwear shirt, shows up and tells the first spokesperson that it is not fair to judge people of the past by the morals of the present. Tell *that* to liberal progressives.

Anyway, the next thing the scientists know, they are back on the plane, and everything is OK; the plane is landing, and the crazy guy who jumped out is back in his seat. Morris and Paxton decide the cloud thing was a dream somehow shared by ESP, giving the doctor a chance to give a brief lecture on ESP to the audience. Endicott thinks it was real and is proven right when the plane lands and it is twenty-four hours late, whereupon Doctor Morris throws his notebook full of the beta bomb calculations in the trash—pseudo-spoiler alert.

But, ah, that's the not the real ending to the movie. The real ending—real spoiler alert—is that thanks to some shared ESP, I followed behind Doctor Morris and retrieved his notebook from the trash and am now building a beta bomb in my basement. But don't worry; I only intend to use it for peaceful purposes.

27

The Second Woman (1950): Hitchcock Lite

This movie opens with a dream sequence narrated by a young woman. In her dream, she looks around and sees a beautiful house on a cliff overlooking the crashing waves. But wait—it is wrecked now and stands only in her memory. And so, still narrating, we go back in her memory to see what happened to the house and the man she loved who lived in it. As her story begins, she is a single, lonely, slightly odd young woman who lives with none other than Florence Bates—more about that later. She will soon meet the man who lives in the great house and fall madly in love with him, only to discover that he has a terrible secret that will change her life forever.

But no, this is not *Rebecca* (1940). This is *The Second Woman*, a Hitchcock rip-off starring Betsy Blake and Robert Young, a year after Young started on *Father Knows Best* on radio and four years before that program transitioned to television. There is a lot of TV in this film; Director James V. Kern served as writer, actor, and director and mostly directed TV sitcoms like *I Love Lucy*, *My Three Sons*, *The Donna Reed Show*, and *My Favorite Martian*. Trying to copy Hitch for this potboiler, Kern apparently found that Lawrence Olivier and Joan Fontaine were too old, and maybe Teresa Wright and Bob Cummings turned it down.

Like other Hitchcock movies, the story starts out with our lovers meeting on a train; he is distant and troubled, yet there is witty dialogue—well, witty for this terrible script—and the shy girl falls head over heels for him, unaware of his *troubled past*. He lives alone in a house on the ocean that we already know was destroyed later. It actually is ultramodern and looks like a cross between Falling Water and the Van Damme house near Mt. Rushmore in a *future* Hitchcock film, *North by Northwest* (1959). Maybe the Master of Suspense got the idea for the house from watching this thing? Nah, I don't think so. The girl lives next door to our hero in a house that *does* look like Manderley with her aunt, played by Bates, who gives a much more subdued performance here than her wonderful role as the repulsive socialite-wannabe Edythe Van Hopper in *Rebecca*.

The girl does have a name in this film, unlike Ms. Fontaine in *Rebecca*, who is never named, except later as Mrs. de Winter. It's Ellen, and she has fallen for the brooding and mysterious architect Jeff. As Jeff, Young is obviously caught between trying to play a dark character in this film and doing his weekly radio show as the lovable and often foolish Jim Anderson. As a result, Young's performance here is weird and disconnected. Maybe that's just as well because the writers of this thing also wanted to channel *another* Hitchcock film, in which our heroine is madly in love with someone who *might* be a psychopath—read: *Spellbound* (1945).

So enter Jeff's *troubled past*: his fiancé, the woman he built the house for, died in a car wreck with Jeff apparently behind the wheel. Soon after Jeff meets Ellen, his luck gets even worse; his dog is poisoned, his prized piece of artwork fades, his horse breaks an ankle while just standing in a stall and has to be put down, he loses his biggest client through a postal error, his house burns down, and Ellen is nearly killed by a speeding car. Everyone tells Ellen that Jeff is nuts and is doing these things to himself as punishment for his fiancé's death. Throughout the nonsense, Kern does his best to copy Hitchcock: The film is beautifully photographed in stark black-and-white noir photography by Academy Award-winning cinematographer Hal Mohr. The running time is filled with brooding *Rebecca*-like music, usually paired with scenes of the surf crashing.

There is even a scene right out of *Spellbound*, where it seems that Jeff, in a trancelike state, may murder Ellen. But like Ingrid Bergman's character in that film, Ellen stands by her—apparently screwy—man, suspecting, against all evidence to the contrary, that Jeff is sane and that someone close to him is doing these things for revenge. But who? Well, there are really only two suspects, and—spoiler alert—it turns out that they are *both* guilty.

In real life, actress Betsy Blake was much more colorful than the goody-goody character Ellen she plays. A survivor of the sinking of the *Andrea Doria*, Blake became the third wife of Hitchcock favorite leading man Cary Grant, who, like Jimmy Stewart, starred in *three* Hitchcock films. Grant, an active bisexual, fathered two children with Blake, and the couple led an alternative lifestyle that included yoga, meditation, open sexuality, and experimentation with LSD.

BTW #1: No, I don't think Hitchcock sat through this thing, but there certainly were a lot of directors who tried to copy him, and he must have been bemused—and at least a little flattered—by the copycats. The most prolific early example was William Castle, who made an entire career "paying homage" to the master; see my review of *The House on Haunted Hill* (1959). There is actually an entire genre of bombs I call *Hitchcock lite*, and *The Second Woman* is only a minor example. One of my favorites is the previously mentioned *Mirage* (1965), in which director Edward Dmytryk casts *Spellbound* star Gregory Peck as an amnesiac who may or may not have killed his boss and is chased around by bad guys looking for a Hitchcock-like MacGuffin: some papers in a briefcase.

BTW #2: *The Second Woman* contains the old bomb device known as the *thank goodness he was only shot in the shoulder* bit. Yes, Jeff is shot in the struggle with the bad guys in the climax— sorry, another spoiler alert—but "only" in the shoulder. In the happy last scene, Jeff is shown wearing a sling, which the kindly doctor tells him he can take off because the bullet only went through the deltoid. That remark lets the film end with a joke because Jeff and Ellen laugh as they confess they don't know what a deltoid is.

Well, I do, and the bullet hole we see in the fight scene is squarely in the back of Jeff's shoulder, nowhere near the deltoid but right on top of the subclavian artery and vein, the brachial plexus, and the cupola (top) of the lung. In real life, such injuries can puncture the lung and lead to massive bleeding and loss of the arm, if not death. So the kindly doctor is quite wrong when he dismisses Jeff's injury as "nothing." But the "just a shoulder wound" thing is common in bombs—see my review of *Highway Dragnet*—and the doctor also spent the entire movie convinced it was Jeff who was the psychopath, so apparently he's wrong a lot.

28

The Alphabet Murders (1965): An Agatha Christie Mystery as a Screwball Comedy

I really don't know what to make of *The Alphabet Murders*; is it a lost gem or an ill-conceived mess? Well, it might be a little of both, but largely forgotten now and widely regarded as a minor cinematic experiment at best, *The Alphabet Murders* certainly fits my definition of a bomb.

Like much of the population of Earth, I am a fan of Dame Agatha. She created great characters, settings, and a collection of wonderful detective protagonists, but unlike Rex Stout, who was really in the writing game for these elements and often cared little for the actual facts of the whodunnit, Christie usually laid out all the clues for the reader and let them exercise their brain, or, as Hercule Poirot would say, their "little gray cells."

Also like a significant fraction of the population of Earth, Poirot, the fussy but brilliant former Belgian policeman, is my favorite Christie detective. I have read all the Poirot short stories and many of his full-length adventures, including *The ABC Murders*, a nice morbid tale, narrated in part by Poirot's Dr.

Watson, Captain Hastings, which follows the exploits of Poirot as he tracks down a serial killer who murders people whose initials are alliterations in alphabetical order: A. A., B. B., C. C., and so on, always leaving a copy of the British ABC Railway guide at the scene of the crime. All clues lead to a miserable, disabled salesman named Cust, who suffers from frequent headaches, but Poirot—semi-spoiler alert—correctly outs the real murderer and motive and even deduces that Cust's headaches are due to his glasses! Certainly, the executives at MGM-Britain had the right to make this neat little mystery into a film, but why in the world did they hire Frank Tashlin to direct?

Tashlin was a comedy writer who worked for Hal Roach Studios—think Laurel and Hardy—before moving on to animate and write for Warner's Looney Toon Cartoons. He worked his way up the Hollywood ladder to direct moves for Bob Hope (e.g., *The Lemon Drop Kid* [1951]), Martin and Lewis (e.g., *Artists and Models* [1955]), the highly cynical *Will Success Spoil Rock Hunter?* (1957), and a number of Jerry Lewis vanity films in the late '50s and early '60s. Near the end of his career, Tashlin directed a silly NASA spy spoof-romance that is one of my guilty pleasures, *The Glass Bottom Boat* (1966). Borrowing from his experience as a 1940s cartoonist, Tashlin's films were known for their screwball stories, slapstick, and sexual innuendo.

So naturally, when MGM-Britain handed Tashlin the job of directing Christie's story, he decided to film it as farce, hiring *Rock Hunter* star Tony Randall to play Poirot as an Inspector Clouseau–like bumbler. Small wonder—United Artists had scored a huge hit with that character three years earlier in *The Pink Panther*. The result: the proper and dashing Capt. Hastings is played by Robert Morley as an overweight buffoon who tangles with an assassin during a silly scene in a steam room and gets locked in a car trunk with an attractive but drunken woman.

The first victim is a clown who does a high-diving act, the murder weapon is a blowgun, and the apparent murderer is a buxom blonde—a Tashlin casting trademark; he paired Randall with Jayne Mansfield in *Rock Hunter*—played by Anita Ekberg.

While Christie actually instilled Poirot with some comic traits, this odd mix of reserved British humor and Tashlin's desperate jokes just doesn't work. I'll say four good things about the film: (1) Randall tries hard, (2) it's fun to see London in the swingin' '60s, (3) Tashlin does deliver an ending that is sort of like the book and reveals Poirot's brilliance, and (4) there *is* one truly funny scene. Walking out of a police station, Randall runs right into Margaret Rutherford, obviously in character as Miss Marple. The two glare at each other with a mutual disdain.

As the movie progresses, a running joke is made of the fact that Morley's beleaguered Captain Hastings goes through one physical humiliation after another, losing his shoes and going without sleep or a shower. He becomes shabby-looking and apparently begins to smell. It would be too mean to say that the same thing happens to this film, but *The Alphabet Murders* is certainly an oddity. As the old saying goes, the book was better than the movie.

29

Teenagers from Outer Space (1959):
The Backstory Was Better

Recently, I was watching an old episode of *Perry Mason* when I noticed that the victim looked familiar. I checked the credits, and sure enough, I was right; it was Bryan Pearson. Seeing Pearson on the small screen compelled me to re-watch his greatest big-screen triumph, *Teenagers from Outer Space* (*TAFOS*). I had not seen it since before I was a teenager myself. Here is my report: it has not improved with age.

The stories are true: *TAFOS* is one of cheapest-made science fiction films of all time. It begins with the landing of a spaceship in some typical scrubby California landscape. All we see of the ship is its top, which looks exactly like a large garbage can lid. In a sequence reminiscent of the Stateroom scene in *A Night at the Opera* (1935)—watch it on YouTube; it's worth it—the thing opens, and out pile four guys wearing '50s-style exercise suits made to look like uniforms by decorating them with strips of duct tape. Three of the aliens are teenagers, and the fourth is their adult leader. You can tell he's the leader because he has more duct tape.

In a bit of exposition, we learn these teenage boys are something right out of Heinlein's *Starship Troopers*—young soldiers who are the product of a mechanistic military society. They have come not to conquer Earth but to use the planet as a breeding ground for gargons, lobster-like creatures that will grow to enormous size after eating enough Earthlings. These aliens grow gargons for food—apparently, they really like seafood.

But one of the boys pulls out his obviously toy ray gun—yes, the prop person really did buy the actors toy ray guns—and tries to force the others not to release the kraken . . . er, gargon. Seems our hero, an alien named Derek (really?), reads books—yikes, no teenagers do that anymore—and has become a cheese-eating pacifist. Another teenager, Thor—now there's an alien name—overpowers Derek, who runs into the nearby town. On orders from the older guy with all the duct tape, Thor gives chase.

In town, goody-goody Derek meets nice girl Betty, and they instantly fall in love. Betty lives with her grandfather, a character known by the original moniker of Gramps. For the rest of the film, Derek repeatedly saves Betty and Gramps from Thor's wrath. Thor is one determined guy; in his efforts to catch up with and capture Derek, he is shot multiple times by police, has the bullets removed without anesthesia, gets all smashed up in a car wreck, and has a fleet of spaceships crash into him. Ouch.

The budget shortcuts taken in this film are legendary. The movie was shot on the streets of LA but with narrowed views to give the illusion of a small town. The ray guns were made to flash by attaching a mirror to them and shining a flashlight on the mirror from behind the camera. Much of the movie was made on silent film—cheaper—and the soundtrack was added later. The house where Betty and Gramps live was used for free when the filmmaker told the owner he was making a student film for UCLA. The ray guns supposedly turn people into skeletons; male, female, or dog, the filmmaker used the same skeleton, borrowed from a high school science classroom, for all the victims. Toward the end of the movie—semi-spoiler alert—the aliens send a convoy of attacking spaceships, an effect created by having the actors look up toward the sky and say something like "Look at all those spaceships!"

Yes, *TAFOS* is stupid and cheap. What's great about it is its backstory. The filmmaker—this movie was a one-person production—was Tom Graeff, who actually did study film at UCLA. Graeff's entire budget was $14,000, which he borrowed from Pearson; Pearson's German-born wife, Ursula; and a guy named Gene Sterling. This film was a cross between a regional film and a vanity project; Pearson was a British actor who immigrated to the United States, met Graeff, and loaned him the money to make *TAFOS* in hopes of building a career here. Boy, did he back the wrong horse.

Graeff then gave roles to friends and payers: he cast Pearson (billed as Bryan Grant) as Thor, Ursula as a secretary, Sterling as the supreme alien leader, and his then-lover (billed, not surprisingly, as David Love) as Derek. The guy with the extra duct tape in charge of the spaceship teenagers is played by King Moody, who actually had a good career on *Get Smart* and as the original Ronald McDonald. Dawn Bender (Betty) also had a fairly decent career on radio. Graeff, billed as Tom Lockyear, also appears in the film as Joe Rogers, a reporter—he has a press card in his hat—who is a completely extraneous character but nonetheless appears in almost half the scenes.

At first, the Pearsons were friends with Graeff, but debt makes enemies; they sued Graeff to get their money back when it became evident that the film was a dud. Eventually, they did get it back, only to discover that Graeff had sold the film to Warner Brothers (!); a judge subsequently ruled that the Pearsons were not entitled to any of the money Warner's made on it. Eventually, the Pearsons divorced and quit acting but apparently not before Bryan got that *Perry Mason* gig.

Graeff fared even worse. He evidently suffered from mental illness and began to believe that he was Jesus Christ. Graeff tried to change his name to "Jesus Christ II" and took out an ad in the *Los Angeles Times* announcing he was Christ and listing churches where he would be preaching. Christian groups protested, and Graeff performed his first miracle by disappearing—to the East Coast. He later returned to LA and took out an ad in *Variety* touting a screenplay that he said was so good he would only sell it for half a million bucks, more than any screenplay had sold for at that time. Graeff was outed as that "Jesus Christ guy" and committed suicide by shutting himself in his garage with the car running. *TAFOS* shows flashes of true creativity, and it is sad and interesting to speculate what Graeff could have done with a real budget.

And Warner's? They fared worst of all. In 1970, tired of paying the license on the film, they let *TAFOS* slip into the public domain. Too bad—the film has become a true cult bomb, and they could have made a mint on royalties.

Fiend Without a Face (1958): How It All Began for Me

Growing up in Portland, Oregon, in the '60s, falls and winters were scary times. First, there was the darkness; located above the forty-fifth parallel, Portland gets only about eight hours of light at the winter solstice, so as a kid, I went to school and came home in darkness. Then there's the weather: cold, rainy, windy all the time. Portland gets about forty or more inches of rain per year, and it comes down constantly. I am a survivor of Portland's famous Columbus Day Storm (1962). The fake weather I saw in the old Universal horror pictures—usually set in "Transylvania"—had nothing over the real weather I was actually living through. Then there were the deaths of people I admired: Pope John XXIII and John Kennedy in 1963, my grandmother in 1964, and so on.

The spooky feeling of darkness and dread that soaked my childhood in the fall and winter months was only exacerbated when I turned on the TV late at night with my dad to see bombs—usually horror films selected with ironic bemusement by whatever local TV host had drawn the short straw and had to stay up late to host *Science Fiction Theater* or whatever. It was on one such program, on a typical stormy night, on the old black and white, that I first saw *Fiend Without a Face* (*FWAF*). When I think of how my interest in bombs started, I think of this film.

Like *Fire Maidens from Outer Space* (*FMFOS* [1956]; see my review), *FWAF* was an independently made British sci-fi B picture. Unlike *FMFOS*, *FWAF* is actually somewhat interesting and fun to watch; I saw it again recently after many years, and it has not lost any of its campy delights.

The producers of *FWAF* chose correctly when they decided to make the film "look American," even though it was filmed in England with a mostly British cast, so that it would appeal to US drive-in audiences. To do this, they set the story in a US-Canadian airbase—there are signs everywhere telling the audience that the base is in Manitoba—and hired American B-movie stalwart Marshall Thompson to play base commander Major Jeff Cummings. Cummings's second-in-command has the all-American name Captain Al Chester. But look carefully at the actor portraying him; he is none other than the—later, openly gay—British child star Terry Kilburn, who played annoying children in such classics as *A Christmas Carol* (1938), in which he took a particularly cloying turn as Tiny Tim, and *Goodbye Mr. Chips* (1939) before growing up but still finding parts such as this. His final movie role was a small part in Stanley Kubrick's brilliant *Lolita* (1964). The rest of the cast are also British actors, including a mob of angry townspeople who could easily have appeared in the Universal monster movies, if they only had pitchforks.

The film provides a lot of stock footage of 1958-era jets flying around to prove that the action is set on an airbase, but the main feature of the airbase is a nuclear reactor; no respectable 1950s sci-fi setting was complete without one. It seems that the airbase is engaged in some top-secret experiments to channel nuclear energy to planes flying at high altitudes or some such hokum. As the movie opens, the area around the airbase is being plagued with mysterious deaths, and the corpses are found with a hole in the base of their necks and their brains and spinal cords sucked out. The angry townspeople were sure that the deaths are somehow linked to the nuclear reactor until Jeff points out that radioactivity does not usually suck the nervous system out of people's bodies.

But, alas, the angry townspeople are sorta right; unbeknown to Jeff, a scientist living nearby the base is experimenting with telekinesis, using electrical shocks to his body to try to turn the pages of a book with his mind. All he was getting from his experiments were body burns when, one day, one of his attempts happened to occur during a surge of nuclear power from the plant. Not only did the book page turn, but the scientist accidentally created a monster, this one invisible and fond of sucking out brains and spinal cords in order to reproduce.

Somehow Jeff gets suspicious of the scientist and goes to call on him, stumbling in on his beautiful assistant, Barbara Griselle, who is, for some reason, taking a shower in the middle of the day and walks into Jeff wrapped only in a towel. This causes Barbara to initially side with the angry townspeople in their mistrust of Jeff and the airbase. The purpose of this scene was apparently to provide the film promoters with a picture of a woman in a towel and a surprised expression on her face to splash all over the movie's posters. Barbara, incidentally, is played by Kim Parker, a prolific B-film actress who survived a Nazi concentration camp as a child to come to England and find work in such films as, coincidentally, *FMFOS*, in which she plays one of the lesser fire maidens.

By the time Jeff and Al figure out what is going on, it is too late; the monsters have taken over the nuclear power plant, killed most of the base crew, and turned up the nuclear power. This leads the monsters to become visible, and they look like—surprise—brains and spinal cords. The monsters, which are the best thing about the film, are wonderful rubber creations that use their spinal cords in a whiplike fashion to creep along and fly through the air—all thanks to great stop-motion photography—to attack their victims.

Trapped in the scientist's house with a few red-shirt-type waste-Os, Al and Barbara and the others shoot it out with pistols as the creatures break in through windows or come down the chimney. Once shot, the creatures die in spectacular fashion, dropping to the ground, deflating, and emitting grape jelly with a gurgling noise. Just as our heroes are running out of ammo, Jeff—spoiler alert—fights his way to the reactor and blows it up, killing all the creatures. The movie ignores the fact that such an explosion would spread nuclear fallout and kill all of Manitoba. Instead, the movie ends with Barbara, who has gone from hating to loving Jeff—such is the way with these films—giving our hero a big smooch.

FWAF, which actually did OK at the box office, was not without its production struggles. Director Arthur Crabtree, who had a respectable career as a director and cinematographer for England's Gainsborough Productions, reportedly walked onto the set on first day of shooting, read the script, and walked off the set. Apparently, Crabtree, who was directing the film as a favor to a friend, was unaware that it was a "monster picture."

His career was in semi-decline by 1958, but I guess he still had his pride. This left Marshall Thompson to direct the film until Crabtree, who apparently needed money more than his pride, returned a few days later.

FWAF has been called one of the "greatest flying brain movies ever." I agree and would add that it is also one of the greatest *dying* brain movies ever.

31

The Skydivers (1963): OK, Maybe Ed Wood Really Wasn't the Worst Director of All Time

One thing about Ed Wood: the man had range. He directed pseudo-documentaries, sci-fi, monster/horror, crime, and, yes, pornography films. Widely regarded as the worst director of all time—see my review of *Jail Bait*—Wood also had competition for that title: a director named Coleman Francis.

Francis also had range but was less prolific; he directed only three films—*The Beast of Yucca Flats* (1961), *The Skydivers* (1963), and *Red Zone Cuba* (1966)—monster, adventure, and spy pictures. All three films had slipped into obscurity until they were all found and lampooned by *MST3000* in the 1990s.

Francis's films had several things in common. They were all filmed around Santa Clarita, California; they all featured a character named Joe (*Red Zone Cuba* had a Joe *and* a Jose); they all centered around the drinking of coffee; and they all featured downbeat stories and violent deaths. Francis's films also featured convoluted plots, tricks to save money, and cameos by the director and his ex-wife. Weirdly, each film contains a scene in which police shoot at fleeing suspected, and sometimes innocent, criminals in a vigilante style. The movies were produced by and starred a heavily decorated Korean War veteran turned B-film actor named Anthony Cardoza (*not* Carbone of *The Last Woman on Earth*). Cardoza also worked with Ed Wood; *The Beast of Yucca Flats* reunited Cardoza with his *Night of the Ghouls* (1959) costar, Swedish wrestler Tor Johnson.

I will not bother to review two of Francis's films here. *The Beast of Yucca Flats* basically involves a defected Russian scientist who hides out in the titular heavily irradiated area of New Mexico and turns into a crazed killer. This putrid film opens with the strangulation of a half-naked woman as she steps out of the shower and hints that the killer rapes her corpse. More than you needed to know. *Red Zone Cuba* follows the incomprehensible exploits of some criminals who get involved with the Bay of Pigs invasion. Both films feature Joes, coffee, and lots of deaths. Again, I view these movies so that you don't have to.

From the start, one can tell that *The Skydivers* is cheaply made, but if you stick with it, you can at least follow the plot, which is downbeat but not putrid. The viewer is also treated to endless footage of a California skydiving troupe performing aerial acrobatics and a Vegas-based guitarist named Dick Bryant playing some pretty impressive electric guitar. The plot? Follow me here: Harry (Cardoza) and his wife, Beth, run a skydiving school. Beth loves and is faithful to Harry, but Harry is fooling around with bad rich girl Suzy, who is the girlfriend of ne'er-do-well mechanic Frankie, who Beth and Harry just fired for drinking on the job. Harry and Frankie duke it out in a prolonged fistfight scene, which ends with Harry promising to stop seeing Suzy if Frankie promises to stay away from the diving school. Thirty minutes into the film, director Francis apparently realized that he hadn't had a violent death yet, so he has one of the skydiving students die in a jump because they didn't open their chute in time.

Enter Joe and the coffee. This time, the Joe is an old Korean War army buddy of Harry's—art imitates life—who comes at Beth and Harry's request to replace Frankie as their mechanic. Within seconds of Joe's arrival at the skydiving school, Beth offers him coffee, whereupon Joe exclaims that he likes coffee. So, he's an alright Joe who likes a cup o' joe. Or is he? Joe soon develops a crush on Beth and steals a kiss. Beth declares she likes Joe but loves Harry. Joe is OK with that, even after a jealous Harry challenges him. So, he is an alright Joe after all. Joe stays platonic friends with Beth, and they drink more joe.

But all is not well. Suzy and Frankie plot to kill Harry, and—spoiler alert—three more violent deaths and an all-around downbeat ending ensue. Along the way, there is more skydiving footage, coffee, and crazed outdoor party dancing; see my review of *The Horror of Party Beach*.

The modern viewer notices two things about this film. First, all the usual cost-cutting tricks are here: heavy use of stock footage to pad running time, silent film with the dialogue added in later, incredible continuity and background errors caused by guerilla filming, and the use of lots of locals to play the extras for free so that they could see their name on the screen—the opening credits are an endless list of people you never heard of. And yes, Coleman Francis and his ex-wife appear in a cameo as spectators. By the way, Coleman had really bad teeth; see my review of *The Yesterday Machine*. In fact, like *The Yesterday Machine*, *The Skydivers* is basically a regional film, a movie made to highlight local people and usually financed in part by them. The party band plays in front of a large poster listing the names of the performers—in case the viewer wanted to hire them, I guess—and there is a long scene played in front of a truck sporting the name of a local barbeque joint that may have catered the film.

The second thing the modern viewer notices is that *The Skydivers* is a great example of '50s and '60s hairdos. Beth has a permanent that never changes shape, even in the wind. Suzy has a bouffant. Harry and Frankie spout mini-pompadours that stay in place even during their fight, and Frankie has a bit of a ducktail. Joe has a flat top with fenders. Well, maybe most viewers won't notice the hairdos, but I did because my grandfather was a barber, and I learned this stuff from the posters in his barbershop.

As I write this review, I am indeed drinking coffee. I like coffee. But I have no desire to go skydiving. Even if I do, I will open my chute in time so that I can go on to watch yet another bomb.

32

The Blue Gardenia (1951): Talent 0, Bombs 1

A review of this list so far made me realize that I was viewing too many films that made the *MST3000* list of bombs because they were so obviously bad and therefore got picked on by that show. So, I thought I'd go back to a film that was not such low-hanging fruit.

In fact, I selected *The Blue Gardenia* because it is not generally recognized as a bomb but fits my definition: old, not well remembered, not particularly great, yet somehow fun to watch. The only things sad about *The Blue Gardenia* are (a) its "happy" ending and (b) that it was a fair waste of talent.

First, there is the director, Fritz Lang—yes, Fritz Lang—the German cinema wunderkind who directed *Metropolis* (1927), *M* (1931), *Scarlet Street* (1945), and *The Big Heat* (1953) and was known as the Master of Darkness. Lang was a brilliant director, but you wouldn't know it from this film, which even he didn't like; he regarded it as "a sour little film of little consequence."

Well, that's not quite fair. After all, Warner's instilled it with fair production values and an interesting cast, which was also a waste of talent. It's just that the story is weird, dated, and fairly improbable. But, then, it's a bomb, so that's the fun of it. The story is your basic lonely-working-girl-gets-jilted-by-her-serviceman-in-Korea-boyfriend-so-she-agrees-to-a-date-with-the-office-wolf-only-to-get-drunk-and-maybe-kill-him-when-he-tries-to-force-himself-on-her story. Anne Baxter—yes, Anne Baxter—playing an LA phone operator named Crystal, is having dinner by herself with her boyfriend's picture, eagerly awaiting his return, and even toasts to it with champagne. The cad "looks on" from the photo frame as she opens his recent letter and discovers that he has fallen for a nurse named Angela. I fell for a nurse named Angela once; I wonder if she was the same one?

Anyway, Crystal drowns her sorrows by meeting ladies' man Harry, played by Raymond Burr, and by downing several Polynesian pearl divers while Harry comes on to her at a restaurant called the Blue Gardenia. He buys her a blue gardenia from the flower girl, and Nat King Cole—yes, Nat King Cole—shows up as the floor entertainment and sings a song written by Johnny Mercer—yes, Johnny Mercer—entitled "Blue Gardenia." I'm thinking that these things are why the movie is entitled *The Blue Gardenia*, but that's just a guess. By the way, look for a split-second shot of Dolores Fuller—see my review of *Jail Bait*—as a woman at the Blue Gardenia's bar.

Watching Raymond Burr in this film is a revelation; Burr struggled most of his life with his weight, his looks, and his homosexuality. Yet here he is, seven years before being cast as Perry Mason, looking almost svelte, very handsome, and playing a Don Juan-type quite convincingly.

Anyway, Harry gets Crystal drunk, takes her to his apartment, and the next thing you know, she has hit him with a fireplace poker—maybe. She wakes up in her bachelorette apartment, which she shares with roommates Ann Southern and Jeff (female—this was way before *Three's Company*) Donnell, to the news that Harry was found dead in his apartment, bludgeoned with a fireplace poker. Did our heroine really kill him? Bet you can't guess.

Regardless, it seems she is safe; Harry's idiot cleaning lady, who apparently never heard of not tampering with evidence, has tampered with all the evidence, cleaning up the scene of the crime before she called the police. That leaves the detective, played by none other than a pre-*Superman* George Reeves, and crusading newspaper reporter Casey Mayo, played by Richard Conte, very little to go on. Casey does discover that the suspect (i.e., Crystal) is blond and wore a black dress. In his newspaper column the next day, Casey dubs her—you guessed it—"the Blue Gardenia."

Eventually, Crystal is reassured by Casey's promises in his newspaper that the Blue Gardenia can come to him, and he will give her protection and legal assistance. Crystal does meet with Casey but tells him that she is not the Blue Gardenia but knows who is and that she is acting on that person's behalf. Two things occur next that only happen in movies like this: Casey (a) believes her and (b) falls for her. So when Detective Reeves follows Casey and arrests Crystal, Casey looks and feels like quite the heel.

But just as it looks like Crystal is going to the big house to fry, a woman named Rose—super-spoiler alert, but it's telegraphed at the beginning of the movie—shows up and confesses. Seems Harry got Rose pregnant—this is 1953, so she doesn't *quite* say that—and then blew her off (no pun intended, really), so she whacked him with the poker after drunken Crystal stumbled off. So it was Rose with the poker in the penthouse. Rose, by the way, is played by Conte's real-life wife at the time, Ruth Storey.

To sum up, *The Blue Gardenia* is an overall waste of a lot

of talent: director, cast, musical writer, and musical performers. "Blue Gardenia" is not even a good song; it is infinitely *forgettable* (pun intended) and sounds like Nat King Cole was making it up as he went along.

The film does have a happy ending but not the one shown on screen. Yes, Casey and Crystal make up, but when the viewer considers that it happens at the expense of Rose, who goes off, abused and pregnant, to prison, the ending doesn't feel that jolly. No, here is the real happy ending: in order to stick around and help Crystal, Casey passes up what was in 1953 an apparently sweet assignment: a front-row seat at an atom bomb detonation in the Pacific Ocean. So apparently Casey does *not* go on to develop thyroid cancer or leukemia.

The Fat Man (1951): He Was No Thin Man

Mystery writer Dashiell Hammett was one of the first writers of true hardboiled private-eye stuff, and film and radio of his era could not get enough of his stories and characters. His character Sam Spade was introduced to the film audience in the persona of Humphrey Bogart (*The Maltese Falcon* [1941]) and continued on radio played by Howard Duff in a successful series called *The Adventures of Sam Spade*, which ran on ABC, CBS, and then NBC for six years. Hammett's second most-famous character, Nick Charles, aka the Thin Man, was actually only the hero of one book and an early draft published in the wonderful collection *Nightmare Town* (2000), but the success of William Powell and Myrna Loy's portrayal of the married Nick and Nora in the incredibly great film *The Thin Man* (1934) led to five sequels.

Nick Charles was likely Hammett's most personal character; like Nick, Hammett was a retired detective, a former Pinkerton, an alcoholic, and possessed a dry acerbic humor that pervaded all his observations. As readers of Hammett know, the Thin Man referred not to Charles—who was, as we say in medicine, a mesomorph—but to the murder victim of the novel and the first movie. However, to build audience connection to the subsequent movie sequels, MGM implied that Nick was synonymous with the name the Thin Man in the movies that followed, just like the Pink Panther came to refer to Clouseau in the sequels and not to the diamond.

Given the popularity of the Thin Man, radio writers at ABC got the idea of creating a character for Hammett's radio fans called the Fat Man, based on the idea of a character modeled after Caspar Guttman, the villain of *The Maltese Falcon*, so famously portrayed in the film by Sidney Greenstreet, only as a good-guy detective.[5] The result was *The Fat Man*, a radio show that ran from 1946 to 1951 and starred an actor with the wonderful name of J. Scott Smart. Smart really *was* fat and spent the early episodes lamenting, probably from personal experience, about the tribulations of being overweight such as having trouble crossing your legs and suspecting that every femme fatale who makes a pass at you is a murderess with an agenda. Initially, the character actually referred to himself only as the Fat Man, but he was eventually given a name: Brad Runyan. Despite his inability to run and jump over things, Runyan did get his man or woman in each episode, occasionally—I'm not kidding—by forcing them down with his girth. Smart was wonderful to listen to, delivering his narration with that dry, cynical Hammett-style wit and using an accent that was a cross between Greenstreet and W. C. Fields.

Given the moderate popularity of the radio show, it was only natural that Hollywood would dream up a movie to show radio audiences Smart in the flesh (no pun intended?). Indeed, Smart on the screen is an imposing figure, and the film is filled with fat jokes: Runyan teaching an admiring crowd of chefs how

---

5   Sidney Greenstreet *did* get to play a good-guy detective on radio, portraying Nero Wolfe (1943-1944).

to cook, trying to get into the tiny MG he rented, and getting up to dance a jitterbug in a restaurant while the woman he is with expresses doubt and then admiration. The last is easily the weirdest scene in the movie, inciting a combination of fear and fascination in the viewer. You keep thinking Smart is going to drop dead from a heart attack, but apparently the man could dance.

The rather thin plot (I really did *not* intend that pun) involves the murder of a dentist and the theft of his dental records on a patient named Roy Clark, years before audiences would have associated the name with the *Hee-Haw* star. Roy, played by a very young and therefore particularly beautiful Rock Hudson, turns out to be one of the members of an armored car robbery gang who was wounded, captured, and released from prison with a bad toothache; I guess this was before prisoners got anything they wanted, including free dental care. Roy goes to see the dentist but can't pay for the work, possessing only the suit of clothes the prison gave him on his release. The kindly dentist waives his fee, but a grateful Roy returns a little while later dressed to the nines with a chauffeured car and a bankroll, and pays him.

All of this is shown in flashback as Runyan uncovers the story, and he also deduces—spoiler alert: correctly—that Roy's sudden wealth was due to his looking up his old robbery partners to get his share of the money and—more spoiler alert—that they then probably killed him, hence the dental record theft. There is a completely unnecessary scene in which Runyan sets fire to a toy truck with a tooth in it to demonstrate to the police that teeth survive attempts to burn a body; gee, I didn't know that. There is also a weird association with the posture of female characters and survivability: Audrey Meadows, playing the dentist's nurse with bolt upright posture and "deadly" seriousness, gets bumped off, while Julie London, playing Roy's girlfriend with terrible round-shoulder posture, emphasized by her strapless evening dresses, survives. The whole thing ends— super-spoiler alert—with a shootout involving famous Ringling Brothers clown Emmett Kelly. No, I'm not kidding. Like most bombs, the film is a curio.

Alas, unlike *The Thin Man*, *The Fat Man* did not have legs (another pun?). Hammett was credited as "creator" of the radio series but I think had little to do with it. He never actually wrote anything about the character, and the film spawned no sequels. Even the director, William Castle, who, in my opinion, was not exactly picky about his material—see my review of *The House on Haunted Hill*—called it "a potboiler of little merit." I'll say these things for *The Fat Man*: the scene of the armored car robbery is exciting and predated Kubrick's *The Killing* (1956) by five years, and Smart is fascinating to listen to and watch. He died nine years later, not of metabolic syndrome but pancreatic cancer—life imitates art: Smart smokes and drinks throughout the film—bringing an end to the character of Brad Runyan.

This odd little film remains as a tribute to the politically incorrect days of yesteryear, but the years have passed, and so have fat jokes. I have a friend who bought a Corvette and another friend who loves Karmen Ghias. I love those friends dearly, and, like Brad Runyan, they are *not* mesomorphs. But like Runyan and his MG, their car choices should not be a source of laughs.

34

Armored Car Robbery (1950):
DA Hamilton Burger as a Ruthless Villain

The last review got me thinking about armored car robbery films. This is actually a subgenre of bombs and non-bombs. Some of the non-bombs include the aforementioned *The Killing* (1956) and the wonderful *The Brinks Job*. The latter is a 1978 movie about the titular real holdup in Boston. The film is decidedly not a bomb; it has a good cast, headed up by Peter Falk; a great director, William (*The Exorcist*) Friedkin; location shooting in Boston; a 75 percent rating on Rotten Tomatoes; and was nominated for an Academy Award.

The bomb category of armored car robbery movies obviously includes the previously reviewed *The Fat Man*. Your intrepid reviewer got to wondering if there was another bomb about an armored car robbery, and after extensive research, I found one, cleverly concealed by the title *Armored Car Robbery*.

This 1950 film is a true bomb by all my criteria: black and white, largely forgotten, weird plot twists, and a short running time of sixty-seven minutes—films like this were to become mere

TV episodes in the years to follow. You could argue that it's not a bomb on the basis of the fact that it was directed by Hollywood legend Richard Fleischer, but what film wasn't? Fleischer, son of Max Fleischer the cartoonist ("Popeye"), directed fifty-six films in thirty years and had a reputation as a reliable director who could direct any film in any genre on any budget. As a result, he was more than busy and directed some all-time great films, including several of my favorites (*20,000 Leagues under the Sea* [1954], *Fantastic Voyage* [1966], and *Tora, Tora, Tora* [1970]), as well as a fair number of bombs.

Armored Car Robbery features none other than *Perry Mason* costar William Talman as Dave Purvis, a criminal mastermind who stops at nothing to carry off a daring armored car heist and get away with the loot: he kills a cop; double crosses his partner, Benny, by two-timing with Benny's wife, Yvonne, and killing him when Benny is shot in the robbery; and eventually gets all of his partners killed or arrested while he and Yvonne try to hightail it to Mexico. In short, Purvis is no Hamilton Burger. But, then, Talman played mostly bad guys in B pictures like this before he was cast in *Perry Mason* as Burger, the frazzled DA who constantly lost against Raymond Burr.

In real life, Talman could also be no Hamilton Burger; arrested for lewd exposure and marijuana possession, he was fired from *Perry Mason* until Raymond Burr was able to get him rehired. To his credit, Talman made public service short films about the dangers of cigarette smoking that were aired posthumously after his death from lung cancer. Talman was one of the first actors to come out publicly against cigarettes, just three years after Surgeon General Luther Terry's famous report.

The short running time of *Armored Car Robbery* is mostly taken up by the heist, which is fairly clever, and the dogged pursuit of the gang by tough-as-nails detective Jim Cordell, who was the partner of the cop Purvis killed and is more than a little upset about it. Cordell is played by ubiquitous character actor Charles McGraw, whose prolific career was cut short when he fell through a plate glass window in his house and bled to death before the paramedics arrived.

Cordell's relentless chase after Purvis nearly costs the life of his new partner, played by Don McGuire. McGuire did not acquire much fame as an actor, but as a screenwriter, he achieved notoriety for such scripts as *Bad Day at Black Rock* (1954) and *Tootsie* (1982).

The film is fast-paced and watchable, but what is hard to accept by today's standards is its treatment of women, who are dismissed and objectified. A "man's" picture, *Armored Car Robbery* features exactly three women. In order, they are as follows:

1. The wife of the cop who is killed. She gets visited by Cordell, and *she* ends up soothing *him* for *his* loss!
2. The girlfriend of Purvis. She is played by Adele Jergens, an actress who usually played girlfriends of gangsters or strippers. Here she plays the girlfriend of a gangster who is also a stripper. She spends half of her screen time strutting around on a stage in a G-rated burlesque outfit to the catcalls and whistles of the audience, including one of the detectives, who detects that she's "a lot of woman."
3. A nurse. At the end of the film, Cordell pays a call to his partner, who is recovering in the hospital. Cordell walks into the room, looks at the nurse, and gives her one of the most remarkable stink eyes you will ever see on film, whereupon she slinks away.

This is one of those misogynist films that could only have been made in the '50s. But, hey, I'm a guy, so I'm willing to overlook all that and tell you that *Armored Car Robbery* is fast-paced, exciting, and has great location shooting in LA, including a no-tell motel that I think was used later in *Guide for the Married Man* (1967), another sexist, misogynist film that I really enjoyed.

I think I'd better quit this review now while I'm behind.

35

The Green Slime (1968):
The Last of the Bullet-Shaped Rocket Movies

In 1968, MGM released two science fiction movies that were historically notable. The first was released in April, the second in December. More about the first film at the end of this review.

The second, made in Japan as a *tokusatsu* (special effects film) with a Japanese director (Kinji Fukasaku), Japanese film crew, and by Japanese companies (Ram and Toei, film studios that released many of the '60s Japanese monster movies), masqueraded as an American film by touting its MGM release and American cast, including English-speaking actors who happened to be living in Japan at the time. These include Robert Horton, playing the square-jawed Commander Jack Rankin; Richard Jaekel, sporting a blond crewcut and looking exactly like John Glenn in his Mercury days, as Commander Vince Elliott; and the beautiful Luciana Paluzzi as Dr. Lisa Benson. You'll remember Paluzzi as the Bond villainess in *Thunderball* (1965) who tries to get Sean Connery killed but is shot by her own henchman.

The film opens with a giant meteorite hurtling toward earth.

The only hope lies in twinkly-toothed all-American hero Rankin flying to the nearby space station, taking over, and assembling a crew, including station commander Elliott and a pacifist doctor (Ted Gunther), to fly onto the meteorite and plant bombs to blow it up. The mission succeeds, but the doc unwittingly brings back the titular goo on his shoe, which begins to grow once the crew is back on the space station. This leads to a grammatical crisis: the posters for the film show a picture of a sexy female astronaut being attacked by a tentacle—there is no such scene in the film—and the caption "The Green Slime Are Coming!" When I saw this, I thought, *Shouldn't that be "The Green Slime Is Coming!"?*

But no, *are* is correct because once the slime gets on the spaceship, it morphs into multiple silly-looking screaming vegetable creatures that feed on their own and human blood and multiply like crazy. They are soon running all over the ship wreaking havoc, while everything poor Commander Elliott tries fails to stop them. This leads Rankin to pull rank (pun intended) and take over again; he apparently does that a lot, the audience is told. This makes Elliott mad, especially since there was already something between the two men. It turns out that the something is not complicated; Rankin used to date Dr. Benson, and now she is Elliott's girl. This leads Rankin to scoff a lot and basically call Elliott a pussy. This makes Elliott madder, and so on.

Of some cultural note, the Japanese audiences had no interest in this stupid and obvious love subplot, so it is omitted completely from the Japanese version of the film, which, as a result, is thirteen minutes shorter and more "exciting." The excitement consists mostly of Dr. Benson and her patients running from section to section of the station while Rankin tries to contain the creatures with sliding doors. In one great scene, the pacifist doctor gets trapped behind one such door with the monsters, and when the door is opened, he is standing there, bled and electrocuted to death and with a very surprised expression on this face.

Eventually—spoiler alert—Elliott dies a hero, Rankin evacuates and then blows up the station with the creatures on it, and Rankin gets the girl and makes a speech about how Elliott was not a pussy after all. I guess that's a happy ending.

The Green Slime is silly and looks cheap, but some have touted it as a predecessor to Ridley Scott's *Alien*—same basic plot. Maybe, but I think the "importance" of the film is this: it was the last of the big-screen bullet-shaped rocket movies. One reviewer noted that the models in the film "lacked detail," and that is an understatement. The obviously toy buildings, rockets, and equipment are recycled cheap-looking stuff from other Japanese monster films. The rockets and space station are straight out of the designs of John Polgreen, who illustrated the children's space books written in the '50s and early '60s by Lester Del Rey. Not only are the designs and costumes childish, but we are treated again, but perhaps for the last time, to bad science, such as normal gravity and sound in space.

Ironically, all of that was to end when MGM released the other film, the one in April: Kubrick's *2001: A Space Odyssey*. Yes, that film actually came out before *The Green Slime*, but either it was too late to stop the latter film's release, or the producers paid no heed. Regardless, *2001* ushered in a new area of sci-fi in which spaceships were not bullet-shaped, models had incredible detail, and space was correctly portrayed as silent, vacuous, and cold. Kubrick's film paved the way for the *Stars Wars* films eight years later, and the bullet-shaped rocket and bad science that had marked prior sci-fi films for decades were gone for good. It's too bad in a way; *hearing* the space station in *The Green Slime* blow up and seeing the debris fall *downward* is one of the many guilty pleasures of a good bomb.

By the way, I realized after this review that despite my best attempts, I slipped up and went back to reviewing bad films lampooned by *MST3000*. Not only was *The Green Slime* featured on that program, but it was actually the subject of the pilot episode.

36

It Conquered the World (1956):
Now I Really Hate Brussels Sprouts

Well, after trying to swear off films lampooned by *MST3000*, I screwed up with the last review, so here I go again. As I mentioned in my review of *The Green Slime*, the screaming vegetable monsters are fairly ridiculous—not to be confused with Fairleigh Dickinson, where my daughter went to school—and the cheap models pretty much sank the film. Those monsters got me wondering what the dumbest, cheapest movie monster was. Just in these reviews alone, there is stiff competition: in addition to the screaming vegetable monsters, there are the gill-faces with the bratwurst in their mouths from *The Horror of Party Beach* and the giant snails from *The Monster That Challenged the World*. Trust me, there are even dumber movie monsters out there, and it's a very crowded and close contest, but according to my extensive research, the winner is: Denny Dimwit.

In the 1956 quickie film *It Conquered the World* (*ICTW*), Roger Corman got the idea of creating a monster from Venus based on *his* extensive research on what was known about the planet at the time. That is, Corman found out that the atmosphere on Venus had high pressure and was toxic to animal life, so he posited that a Venusian would be a short vegetable. He created something that has been variously described as a three-foot-tall pear, pickle, or cucumber and had motorized tree branch arms. I vote for a giant Brussels sprout, especially since I don't like Brussels sprouts—unless they are deep fried in tasty batter like some restaurants make them, but I digress. The thing had a goofy sneer and teeth jutting out everywhere that made it look like an evil Mortimer Snerd. When the cast saw it, they laughed, and the writer named it Denny Dimwit. Actress Beverly Garland reportedly kicked it and said, "*That* conquered the world?"

Corman had to admit that maybe it was a *little* small, a situation he remedied by placing it on a table. The table had wheels, so Denny could be moved by a prop guy who climbed behind him and pushed him back and forth. That was the only way Denny moved; one day into shooting, his mechanical arms broke.

Thanks to silly writing, choppy editing, and poor production values, the plot of *ICTW* is fairly incomprehensible, but here it goes: Denny comes to Earth from Venus and communicates by radio with a disillusioned scientist, Dr. Tom Anderson, played by a young Lee Van Cleef, ten years before his (in)famous turn as Clint Eastwood's nemesis in *The Good, The Bad, and The Ugly* (1966). Denny convinces Tom that he should help him get mind control of Earthlings to keep them from destroying one another. Tom helps Denny send out mind-control devices enclosed in cheap-looking rubber bats, the flying kind, and soon everyone in the picture except for Tom; his wife, played by Garland; Tom's friend Dr. Paul Nelson, played by a pre–*Mission Impossible* Peter Graves, who starred in a lot of such terrible sci-fi films; and a squad of soldiers, which includes two Corman comic favorites, Dick Miller and Jonathan Haze, is either under Denny's control or killing people who aren't.

Somehow Denny also manages to neutralize all the electric power in the world, an idea obviously stolen from *The Day the Earth Stood Still*, leaving the heroic Dr. Nelson trying to stop him while riding around on a bicycle. Eventually, Dr. Nelson convinces Dr. Anderson that having a creature from Venus wreak all this havoc is not the solution to humanity's problems, and Dr. Anderson goes after the monster with a blowtorch. Spoiler alert—but no surprise—it does not end well for either one of them, leaving Dr. Nelson to deliver a long, boring soliloquy about how humanity's problems can only be solved by people, not three-foot-tall vegetables from Venus. This speech is an early example of Corman existentialism, something he would perfect later in such films as *The Last Woman on Earth* (1960); see my review. The speech is also somewhat trivial, given the fact that the only person left alive to listen to it is Dick Miller.

This film is also an example of typical 1950s misogyny; without a sexy leading lady to promote, Corman kills off all the female characters in the film: they are shot, strangled, or killed by the monster. Given all this, I was surprised to learn that *ICTW* was liked by critics; Leonard Maltin called it "a neat little film," and the thing has an 80 percent *critic* rating on Rotten Tomatoes. However, normal people like me (i.e., not professional critics) know it stinks like those rotten vegetables you bought two months ago and put in your crisper, swearing you were going to start a healthier diet; its *audience approval* rating on Rotten Tomatoes is 30 percent.

Still, this is the best film about vegetables from Venus you are likely to find. It did not improve my opinion of Brussels sprouts, unless they are deep—oh, never mind.

37

Cat-Women of the Moon (1953):
Not All Bad—It's Got Music by Elmer *Bernstien*

I promise I will get off the bad '50s sci-fi kick, but I can't resist one more: 1953's *Cat-Women of the Moon*, an "independent-ly made" moon-flight cheapie produced by B-film mogul Al Zimbalist, no apparent relation to Efrem Zimbalist Jr. of *The FBI* fame. Originally made in 3D, this classic bomb opens with a spaceship set constructed from corrugated fiberglass panels, unmatched office furniture, and old radio sets. As the film be-gins, our five intrepid astronauts, four men and one woman, all dressed in casual work clothes, are going through g-force accel-eration while a voice on the radio constantly begs them to "come in!" You'd think that mission control would have known they were busy during takeoff going through the g-force thing.

Eventually, they recover, answer the radio, and lounge around on the office furniture while starting their "ten-hour trip to the moon." Wow. This is yet another moon-rocket bomb in which all the science is wrong: normal gravity, sound in space, and air on the moon—the astronauts carry matches, cigarettes, and guns. The cast includes Captain Sonny Tufts, a "veteran" of a bunch of WWII movies; a young Victor Jory; and the remarkable Marie Windsor—more about her later.

The plot is so stupid I am not going to go into too much detail. Suffice it to say that our intrepid explorers are soon to find out that the dark side of the moon, the only side that can be inhabited, you see—the light side is so hot that their matches burst into flame—houses a dying civilization of cat women who are "far advanced" over mere Earthlings. They have telekinetic powers and can disappear and rematerialize in different parts of the cheap sets that were obviously left over from some low-budget Roman movie. Turns out that the cat women have hypnotized Ms. Windsor into bringing her crew into their lair so that they can steal the rocket ship and fly to Earth, where they will take over the planet by controlling all the women because they have all the power. Well, they got that part right.

But they didn't count on he-man Victor Jory—yes, Victor Jory—who is always grabbing Ms. Windsor and kissing her, which breaks the cat women's spell because he is such a macho man (!). Also, for such an "advanced race," the cat women's plan to steal the rocket is pretty dumb, and—spoiler alert but not really—it fails. Part of their plan involves sitting with the male astronauts one-on-one and making casual conversation with them over food and wine, in a scene that comes across as a boring segment from a reality TV show about speed dating. The plan also involves the cat women doing some kind of weird modern dance for the men, which looks like the Grecian urn dance from *The Music Man* (1962)—"One Grecian urn . . ." This scene was obviously inserted to (a) feature the dancing "skills" of the Hollywood Cover Girls, a dance troupe that plays the cat women by donning cat makeup and black leotards, and (b) burn up some of the running time. Even at sixty-three minutes, the film drags.

There are three things I found interesting about *Cat-Women of the Moon*, and none of them involves the actual film. First, the movie was clearly the influence for the farce *Amazon Women on the Moon*, a 1987 send-up of late-late TV, which includes a lovingly detailed mockery of a black-and-white '50s sci-fi film. I remember well how, watching these old films on the TV with my dad and brothers, we were treated to choppy segments of the film interrupted by a constant barrage of stupid commercials. Finally, late into the evening, there would be the inevitable announcement that "there will be no further commercial interruptions," which was usually followed by another commercial interruption. *Amazon Women on the Moon* has stupid skits and is no masterpiece, but it got those details right.

Second, there is Marie Windsor. An interesting-looking person, she stood almost five-ten, towering over many of the leading men of her day. As a result, directors often had to use gimmicks to make her appear shorter than the male actors. A close look at *Cat-Women of the Moon* reveals that her male leads are often standing on steps when next to her, and other scenes of her standing next to her male costars are shot from the waist up, likely to hide the fact that some of them may have been standing on lifts. Fortunately, she was never paired with Alan Ladd; it was rumored that the diminutive Ladd had to stand on a box for some of his scenes with Jean Arthur in *Shane* (1953), and she was shorter than Windsor. Interestingly, in Stanley Kubrick's *The Killing* (1956) the director purposely paired Windsor with Elisha Cook Jr.—see my reviews of *Dark Mountain* and *The House on Haunted Hill*—who was five inches shorter than Windsor, likely to emphasize the henpecked nature of the doomed George Peatty, the character Cook was playing.

Third, *Cat-Women of the Moon* actually features a soundtrack by Elmer Bernstein, the Hollywood musical genius who scored

The Magnificent Seven (1960) and *The Great Escape* (1963) and won an Oscar, a Tony, *and* an Emmy. Why? Seems that Bernstein once scored music for a play linked to communist backers. Hauled in front of the House Un-American Activities Committee, Bernstein refused to cooperate, was blacklisted, and his assignments were subsequently downgraded to bad sci-fi films. As an added insult, the credit writers for *Cat-Women of the Moon* even misspelled his name as Elmer *Bernstien*, but it was probably a good thing for his career, which most definitely bounced back. The same cannot be said for the film, which is a true bomb in the late-late bomb arsenal.

38

Whirlpool (1950): Yes, Pauline Kael Was Right

I am no professional movie critic, and I have no cred in that department, but I can certainly admire a critic or two. My favorite film critic is Pauline Kael (1919–2001), the *New Yorker* film reviewer known for her acerbic, biting, and witty reviews and for having a tendency to disagree with her fellow critics, especially when they embraced en masse some movie that she did not like. I, too, am a person who often finds myself in the minority opinion with colleagues, so I can relate to Ms. Kael's single-mindedness and willingness to speak up when the cinematic emperor had no clothes.

Her career in print actually began when Kael was overheard by a magazine editor discussing a film in a coffee shop. The editor offered her the assignment of reviewing Charles Chaplin's *Limelight*, which she subsequently called *Slimelight* in her write-up. Years ago, I was gifted her book *5001 Nights at the Movies*, and I confess that I have almost memorized parts of it, especially those reviews that ran counter to conventional accolades for certain films. For example, I grew up a sci-fi geek and total nerd, and in 1968, I found myself waiting excitedly for the Portland premier of Kubrick's *2001: A Space Odyssey*. I trotted down dutifully with my geek friends to the Hollywood Theater on Sandy Boulevard to see it. Like most viewers, I was blown away by the Cinerama and groundbreaking special effects—see my review of *The Green Slime* (1968)—but I came away marveling at how incomprehensible and downright stupid the plot was. I found myself in the minority opinion until, years later, I read Ms. Kael's no-holds-barred review and discovered that she had the honesty to say just what I had always thought.

Another example: In 1965, I was in Catholic school, and our class took a field trip to downtown Portland's Orpheum Theater to see *The Sound of Music*. While the girls in my class *ooh*-ed and *ahh*-ed and sang along, I sat there in the dark wondering what it was that made me uncomfortable about the movie. I had my a-ha moment when I read Ms. Kael's review; she noted that Christopher Plummer went through the entire film with a wry smirk on his face and "seems to be in a different movie altogether." That was it!

So it was that I came across her review of *Whirlpool* (1950), and it prompted me to see the film. This movie, like *The Blue Gardenia*, is celluloid proof that great talent does not necessarily make for a great, or even good, movie. Directed by Otto Preminger, written by Ben Hecht, and starring Gene Tierney—who, at the time, was proclaimed "the most beautiful woman in Hollywood"—the film obviously had great promise. Yet Ms. Kael called it "a real stinker," berating the implausible story and the silly plot twists. By the way, the music in *Whirlpool* was conducted by Alfred Newman, who wrote my favorite movie score for a film I liked, *How the West Was Won* (1962). Ms. Kael called it *How the West Was Lost*, so I don't always agree with her.

So here is my report on *Whirlpool*: it's a bomb. Ms. Tierney plays a wealthy socialite who is a kleptomaniac and steals from all the best stores in town apparently because her rich psychiatrist husband, played by Richard Conte, two years away from forgoing that front-row seat to an atom bomb blast—see my review of *The Blue Gardenia*—has put her on an allowance. The cad! By the way, my wife's cousin, who is from Spain, has a husband named Rich, and the cousin calls him "my Rich husband" because of issues with translation. But, then, her English is far better than my Spanish, and I digress.

As the film opens, Tierney's character gets caught shoplifting but is saved from being prosecuted by a smooth-talking hypnotist played by Jose Ferrer, who was perhaps ten times better in *The Caine Mutiny* (1954). For that matter, Ms. Tierney was ten times better in *Laura* (1944), made by the same director. The difference here, rather obviously, is that the actors are stuck with a script full of stupid drivel delivered at a breathless pace, which is apparently supposed to pass for clever dialogue. Amazingly, Hecht was one of Hollywood's most acclaimed screenwriters; he won two Academy Awards, hit the rapid-fire/witty dialogue bullseye with his play and film *The Front Page* (1931), and contributed to the scripts of many great movies including *Gone with the Wind* (1939). When you are that prolific, you are going to have a few bombs—it's just math—and his bomb list includes this movie and the 1968 version of *Casino Royale*, which he wrote as an unfunny spy spoof.

Anyway, Mr. Ferrer offers to cure Ms. Tierney of her insomnia and kleptomania with hypnotism. Seems her husband is not that much of a psychiatrist—he knows nothing of her mental issues. Ironically, the pseudo-psychiatry and mental anguish of Ms. Tierney's character in *Whirlpool* was overshadowed by her real-life mental illness; Tierney suffered from severe depression, made a rather public and publicized suicide attempt, was in and out of mental institutions, and received twenty-seven courses of electroshock therapy.

At first, it seems the hypnotist is an OK guy who genuinely wants to help Tierney's character with all her assorted DSM-4 diagnoses—look it up—but no. In reality, his offer of help is all part of his plan to kill someone and frame Ms. Tierney for the murder with the aid of hypnotism, a glass with her prints on it, and her scarf. Meanwhile, he gets himself an iron-clad alibi—wait for it—he has his gallbladder removed. This was in the days when people were hospitalized for weeks after such an operation, and Ferrer performs self-hypnosis on the night of his surgery to block his sensation of pain, slip out of his hospital bed, and commit the murder.

But this film was made in the post-Hays Code era, and the audience knows that Ferrer will not get away with it. He is suspected by a detective played by ubiquitous character actor Charles Bickford, who is resentful because his sweet and kind wife died after a gallbladder operation, while slimy Ferrer is apparently fine. But in an ending scene that is so unbelievable it needs to be seen—spoiler alert—Ferrer bleeds to death, and justice is served.

What was the word Ms. Kael used? Oh yeah: *stinker*.

39

She Devil (1957): Another Term for *Cult Film* Is *Bomb*

Movie Critic Pauline Kael's dry and acrid wit opened the door for other reviewers, such as Roger Ebert, to exercise their comedic chops. While I think Ebert, who was himself responsible for making a pretty bad bomb, *Beyond the Valley of the Dolls* (1970), could be a suckup to too many filmmakers, he was able to publish *three* volumes of negative reviews that were full of witticisms: *I Hated, Hated, Hated This Movie* (2000), *Your Movie Sucks* (2007), and *A Horrible Experience of Unbearable Length* (2012). In the middle tome, he says of one film that "it does not improve on the sight of a blank screen viewed for the same amount of time" and of another, "the negative should be cut up to make mandolin picks for the poor."

That pretty much sums up how I felt about *She Devil*, a film that sets women's and patients' rights back about a hundred years. Every once in a while, you come across a bomb like this one about which someone, sometimes Ebert, has written that it has "achieved status as cult film." I have always wondered what that means; is it a good thing or a bad thing? I personally believe that watching a film that has been branded a *cult classic* is like getting a kiss from someone with bad breath: it's supposed to be a good thing, but it ends up being unpleasant.

So it is that when someone tries to say something nice about *She Devil*, they often call it a *cult film.* Closely based on *The Adaptive Ultimate*, a short story by American sci-fi writer Stanley G. Weinbaum published in 1935 in *Astounding Stories*, *She Devil* involves pseudo-science—what Ebert used to call "woo-woo"—that includes a formula that cures animals of diseases and injuries. It is derived from fruit flies because, as the scientists remind us in the movie, fruit flies can adapt to their environment, and curing disease is just a matter of adapting to it! The formula has been developed by the young and handsome Dr. Scott, played by Jack Kelly, the future mayor of Huntington Beach, California, who proudly shows a string of animals he has cured of various ailments to his older mentor, Dr. Bach—Albert Dekker, who played the titular character in *Dr. Cyclops* (1940). The scene is almost laugh-out-loud ridiculous; Dr. Scott begins with mice and goes to progressively larger animals. He doesn't quite get to a sperm whale, but he comes close.

The next step, the excited Dr. Scott tells Dr. Bach, would be to experiment on humans. Dr. Bach points out that some may see that as unethical, but maybe if they found someone who was going to die anyway . . . And so they do: a pathetic end-stage tuberculosis patient named Kyra. They have her sign a release form, inject her with the serum, and—*voilà*—she is transformed into a healthy and buxom siren who is literally a mankiller. Kyra is played by Mari Blanchard, a '50s/'60s-style pneumatic blond bombshell—see my *Hillbilly* movie reviews—who played femme fatales for a living. Kyra decides she wants to spend her new life doing what she wants, not what others—including the two doctors, who constantly remind her they know what's best for her—tell her to do. She is . . . well, right. Unfortunately, the serum has some unforeseen side effects not listed in the package insert (look it up). It has rendered Kyra impervious to injury and, oh yeah, made her a psychopath. She goes about getting what she wants using robbery, bunko (look it up), and murder. Kyra reminds the doctors they made her this way by experimenting on her with a serum that had unknown side effects, and she is . . . well, right.

But in the world of this movie, men decide what is right, and the doctors decide that what she needs is to have her pineal gland removed; don't ask—more woo-woo. They pump her room full of CO_2 until she passes out. At this point, director Kurt Neumann had a choice how to end the story. In the original short story, Kyra undergoes the surgery and is cured of her sociopathy. Her beauty fades, but no matter—Dr. Scott still loves her. Aw, gorsh. On the other hand, the radio version of this story, aired on *Escape* in 1949, has the doctors deliberately killing Kyra with the CO_2. Neumann, who specialized in downbeat endings (e.g., he directed *The Fly* [1958]), went with a downbeat ending: the removal of Kyra's pineal gland causes her TB to return, and she dies of that. Such is the fate of women who want to be independent and also question unethical medical research.

Like any good bomb, *She Devil* has some fun stuff to notice. Here are two things: First, Dr. Bach's sassy housekeeper is played by none other than Blossom Rock, who played Grandmama in the wonderful *Addams Family* TV series (1964–1966). Second, for two "brilliant doctors," Dr. Bach and Dr. Scott demonstrate some lousy skills: they can't pronounce medical words like *pineal* (*pine-eel*) or *hypertrophy* (*hi-per-tro-phee*), and they view chest x-rays that are supposedly of Kyra but are those of a male and are often displayed backward, something I had not seen since Richard Conte's famous "big casino" scene in *Ocean's Eleven* (1960). I suggest two scientific formulas for the brilliant doctors:

1. The number of times your movie is called a *cult film* is directly related to how stupid it is.
2. Cult film status × stupidity = bombness.

40

Machete (1958): A Rather Dull Reunion

Once again, the Venn diagram comes through. By reuniting elements of other bombs I have reviewed previously—(1) director Kurt Neumann and actors Mari Blanchard and Albert Dekker (all involved in *She Devil* [1957]); (2) Puerto Rico and the Caribe Hilton (*The Last Woman on Earth* [1960]); and (3) actor Lee Van Cleef (*It Conquered the World* [1957])—one comes up with a serious bomb, 1958's *Machete*.

Another United Artists film that opens with the arrival of a DC-6 (see my review of *The Flight That Disappeared* [1961]), this plane lands in San Juan—with great stock footage of El Morro from the air—carrying Don Luis (Dekker), a wealthy sugar plantation owner, and his new and much younger bride, Jean (Blanchard). They are happy for a couple of seconds, but then Jean finds herself getting recognized by guys who look like grownup frat boys, first at the airport and then at the Caribe Hilton. These chance meetings are all despite the fact that Jean has apparently never been to Puerto Rico before. Yep, she's that kind of girl.

Jean, who struts through the film wearing some racy outfits, her Maidenform doing double duty—sorry—does not want Don Luis to think she married him for his money, which everyone in the audience and in the movie, except for Don Luis, knows she did. So, she insists they check out of the Caribe and go straight to the Luis' palatial plantation—say *that* three times fast. Alas, there the ogling only gets worse; Jean meets Luis's three top staff members: plantation overseer Bernardo, a surprisingly good role for a Black actor in 1958 and played by the distinguished Juano Fernenadez, who was actually from Puerto Rico; the oily-as-ever Mr. Van Cleef as Miguel, a parasitic cousin of Luis; and Luis's protégé, Carlos, played by a guy who actually was named Carlos (Carlos Riveras). Riveras was a half-German, half-Mexican actor whom Hollywood used to play that "foreigner" casting trick: he portrayed "foreign-looking people"—Asians, Latins, Indigenous Americans, men from the Middle East, whatever—in many and often much better films such as *The King and I* (1956), *Topaz* (1969), and *True Grit* (1969).

The moral of the film seems to be this: machetes are sharp and can be dangerous. Because the story is set on a sugar plantation, there are machetes everywhere, including one hanging on a wall in Luis's house like a trophy, apparently for the sole purpose of having the characters stab each other with it. Miguel, who is jealous of Carlos, gets drunk and uses it on Luis, and Luis ends up in bed to recover. The observant bomb viewer such as myself notices that between the plane ride, the debacle at the Caribe Hilton, and the machete wound, poor Luis never does get to consummate his marriage on his wedding day.

But, believe it or not, Miguel is not in trouble with Luis for very long. Instead, between Miguel's shady ploys and Jean's promiscuity, the tables instead turn—thanks to a truly ridiculous series of events—on the too-nice-to-be-real Carlos, who is soon exiled by his girlfriend and Luis. But it all ends "happily"—

spoiler alert—with Carlos killing Miguel in a—what else?—machete fight and gold-digger Jean getting roasted in a sugar-cane fire. Once again, director Neumann displays the misogyny that penetrated most of his films such as *She Devil*: the femme fatale gets raped by her husband—so much for the honeymoon—and must die in the end. That leaves Bernardo, Carlos, and Luis to rekindle their bromance without those pesky Jean and Miguel characters around.

The title of *Machete* was later used by Quentin Tarantino and Robert Rodriguez for a fake trailer in their film *Grindhouse* (2007). Trust me; the title is all they used. The goody-goody character of Carlos is at no risk of being confused with anyone played by Danny Trejo. The older *Machete* meets all my definitions of a bomb: a movie usually filmed in black and white that is late-late-night insomnia fare and would likely have been forgotten. The occasional bomb gets resurrected for three reasons: (1) as a cult classic—see my review of *She Devil*, (2) by the film snob elite—see my review of *Detour* (1945), or, (3) in the case of *Machete*, for its title.

At first glance, *Machete* seems to have a longer running time (seventy-five minutes) than most bombs, but don't let that fool you: easily a third is made up of local dancers and musicians performing—it's a bit of a regional film, as the opening credits tell you—and exciting stock footage of sugar-cane mills in action. As I mentioned in my review of *The Last Woman on Earth* (1960), my wife has a lot of family in Puerto Rico. Yes, they own sugar-cane land, and it's fun to see what the island looked like in 1958–1960 (i.e., back when it was nicer). Her family are nice people, but like all real people, they do occasionally have disagreements. Fortunately, they don't have machetes lying around everywhere.

41

The Walking Target (1960):
I Wonder Where They Got the Title From?

In the opening minutes of this movie, the warden tells Nick, the prisoner he is releasing, that he's a walking target. I have a sneaking suspicion that's why the film is titled *The Walking Target*.

The warden makes another prediction: as soon as Nick walks out, every policeman and every tape recorder will be on him. So, sure enough, as soon as Nick walks outside the walls of the prison—the California State Prison, according to the phony sign—there they are: police and tape recorders . . . and also newspaper folk, photographers, and gold-digging girlfriends. They come up to Nick faster and faster, and he beats them off, like the scene where Robert Stack walks into the airport in *Airplane!* (1980).

Seems that the reason Nick (Ronald Foster—nah, you never heard of him) is a walking target—hmm . . . wonder if that's where they got the title—is because he has just served five years for a robbery, and he is the only one who knows where the money is stashed. I do not think this film was made before the days of marked bills, plea bargains, parole officers, and radios in police cars, but all of those things are simply left out to allow for this improbable story to get through the audience's manure detector.

In fact, it's fun to watch the insipid story unfold as a bunch of B-film and TV character actors you also never heard of play dogged policemen, crooked "friends," relentless paparazzi, and evil gangsters, all following Nick around—did I mention that he's a . . . never mind. A flashback attempts to convince us that Nick had a soft spot for his dimwitted partner, Sammy Russo, played by Norman Alden, whom you *will* recognize from his many supporting roles. What we really see in the flashback is that Nick bullied and beat Sammy and had the hots for his wife, Gail, so the idea that Nick now has a heart of gold and wants to make things right by Sammy is a little hard to swallow.

Gail, who is now a widow—seems Sammy was killed trying to get away from the police—is played by Joan Evans, who actually gets top billing in the movie. That's only fair since this film was her last screen credit; Evans stopped acting in films after this flick—"But she was doing so well!"—and began a new career as a journalist for *Photoplay* magazine.

Even though the audience has suspended all belief, we also know the truth: Nick still has a thing for Gail, and the director is trying to work some romance into a film that would otherwise be an argument for celibacy. By the way, this junk was directed by Edward L. Kahn, who directed many *Our Gang* comedies and edited films like *All Quiet on the Western Front* (1930) before making a left turn into grade-Z films like *Flesh and the Spur* (1956) and *Dragstrip Girl* (1957).

Anyway, during the long flashback sequence, Nick realizes that Gail, who has disappeared without a trace, is likely hiding out in a town called Gold City, Arizona, where she grew up and used to run the family diner. I looked it up—there is no such place, although Louis L'Amour did invent such a town for one of his books. Anyway, off Nick goes to Gold City because he, of course, wants to do right by Sammy's widow. Sure. Also, oh yeah, he (a) still has the hots for her and (b) stashed the money in the frame of her car.

Since, as I already mentioned twice, the audience of this movie needs to completely suspend their belief systems to even watch it, it comes as no surprise that Gail still has the car after five years. I was hoping she'd had it crushed into a cube or something. But no, Nick arrives in Gold City to find Gail, the family diner, and the car all still there. Gail is working at the diner with a family friend who is a lanky guy named Lank—get it? Soon, Nick has convinced Gail that he *does* have a heart of gold— maybe it's from being in Gold City . . . oh, never mind—and is going to turn the money over to the police. That makes good girl Gail kiss Nick and profess her love for him. So much for Sammy.

But, alas, standing in the way of this happy ending—spoiler alert—is a showdown with all those people (phony friends, gangsters, dogged police, etc.) who have been following Nick because, as you may not have realized, he is a walking target. Seems that even though it took Nick insider information and a flashback to realize that Gail was hiding out in Gold City, it just sorta occurred to everyone else.

The seventy-four-minute running time does not allow for much follow-up after the showdown; I *think* I saw poor Lank get shot, but I'm not sure he was killed. One of the bad guys, played by Berry Kroeger, definitely gets shot and killed. By the way, both Kroeger and Alden appeared in *Tora! Tora! Tora!* (1970), a movie that was arguably better and definitely longer—twice as long—as this one. Also, *Tora! Tora! Tora!* had a cast of approximately one million people, so it's actually sort of surprising that it starred only two people from *The Walking Target*. As I tell my kids, that's just math.

Also, during the final showdown, one of the policemen gets shot, and it looks bad, but he actually gets better, climbs into a chair, and has the closing dialogue with Nick. Yes, of course I was reminded of the "I'm getting better!" scenes in *Monty Python and the Holy Grail* (1975), a film that was *more* believable than this one.

42

The Cat Burglar (1961): The Long and Short of It

When I think of movies about cat burglars, two come to mind. The first is Hitchcock's 1955 film *To Catch a Thief,* based on a pretty good book of the same title by author David Dodge, featuring a skilled cast led by Cary Grant and Grace Kelly, gorgeously filmed in Technicolor and VistaVision, and with cinematography by the great Robert Burks. The movie was nominated for five Academy Awards (winning one), has a 96 percent "fresh" rating on Rotten Tomatoes, and runs 105 minutes.

And then there's the other one. Like *Armored Car Robbery* (see my review), the other film has a less creative title and is a genuine bomb: black and white, largely forgotten, with a TV actor cast and a sixty-five-minute running time. The running time is not the only thing about *The Cat Burglar* (1961) that seems short. The "good" characters are physically short; the film is short on character development; and the director, William Witney, was obviously short on the budget.

To take the last point first, *The Cat Burglar* opens with one of those continuity mistakes that is born of having a low budget. A cat burglar is prowling on the roof of what we are led to believe by the fake signs is an apartment building. It is obviously a motel; the doors are close together and separated by just one window, and all the windows have identical lamps. After some prolonged prowling, our (anti-)hero settles on the "apartment" of a legal secretary named Nan. Once he breaks in, burglar Jack is in a spacious indoor set with multiple front rooms and windows and more than one lamp.

The low-budget tricks continue. While Jack is looking through drawers that are obviously empty, Nan comes home with a suitcase and a briefcase. She takes a G-rated shower while Jack hides, and when she is fully involved in the shower, Jack grabs the briefcase and runs.

Other money-saving ploys become apparent to the bomb expert such as myself: the characters go through few if any costume changes, and no music was composed that matched what was going on onscreen. Instead, the producers made use of the fact that this was the Beatnik Era to save money; a mind-numbing jazz score plays throughout the entire film. Jack is the taciturn antihero type who mumbles a lot of Maynard G. Krebs stuff like *cool* and *dig it*, which saved the cost of hiring any screenwriters to write coherent dialogue, and wears the same colorless tight-fitting beatnik outfit through the entire film, complete with a leather cap; he looks like he should be reciting beat poetry in a Greenwich Village coffee shop.

I'm hip, daddy-o, to other ways the cats who made this flick saved some bread. The bad guys all wear identical *The Man in the Grey Flannel Suit* (1956; one of my favorite films—check it out) type of dark clothes: Huntsman suits—look it up—black ties, and dark glasses. Most of the action occurs in those wooden garden apartments that were a setting of so many movies; I have already mentioned *He Walked by Night* (1948; see my review) and *Guide for the Married Man* (1967). Apparently, permits to film around those LA buildings came cheap or were free. At one point, Nan is seen driving away in a car filled with movie equipment. Seems the actors had to double as grips too.

The "good" characters, Nan and Jack, are physically short: Nan is played by the diminutive June Kenney, who stood five-foot-two on a hot day. Kenney, who was fairly pretty, is the only character allowed any costume changes. She might have worn her own clothes from home, possibly paid for by money she earned in other B pictures, including the wonderfully named Roger Corman super-cheapie *The Saga of the Viking Women and Their Voyage to the Waters of the Great Sea Serpent* (1958). Jack is played by TV actor Jack Hogan, who was PFC Kirby in the '60s series *Combat!*. The film tries to develop some chemistry between Nan and Jack but comes up, well, short; they seem to be in different movies. Nan gushes about how there must be some good in Jack—what? where?—while Jack mumbles his incoherent beatnik stuff. There are only two scenes that even allow for character development, one in which Jack is getting beaten up and another where Nan is being held with a knife to her throat.

And so, with little understanding of what motivates anyone in the film, the short running time quickly brings the audience to the concluding scene, which occurs on another cheap set. It's supposed to be an abandoned warehouse, but it's just a studio backlot building housing gangplanks for stunt people to fall from and empty cardboard boxes for them to land in.

This is yet another example of how many bombs simply waste talent; *The Cat Burglar* was written by Leo Gordon, an ex-con turned writer and actor who produced some great tough-guy scripts for Jack Nicholson, Charles Bronson, and many others. Quentin Tarantino called director Witney "one of the greatest action directors in the history of the business" and lists four movies as evidence of that. Suffice it to say, this film is not one of them. Instead, despite the collaboration of Witney and Gordon, all this movie gives us are pulled punches and stuntmen falling into those cardboard boxes.

Yes, *The Cat Burglar* comes up short. I didn't even mention the plot, so here's the short version: that briefcase Jack took contained stolen government documents that Nan was unknowingly carrying for her (tall) lawyer boss and the two (tall) spies in those Huntsman suits, whom the boss works with. Jack is no John Robie; he had no clue about the contents of the case. Nan and Jack spend the movie figuring that out and then running from the bad guys, ending up in the warehouse. Film aficionados will recognize that this plot has been stolen from the infinitely better *Pick-Up on South Street* (1953), a Richard Widmark Cold War movie involving a pickpocket who discovers that he has stolen military secrets from the pocket of a spy. Check it out; that movie is cool, baby, and you'll dig it.

43

Behind Green Lights (1946): Bombs Can Be Fun

Every once in a while, you find a film that meets all of my classic requirements for a bomb—black and white, short running time, largely forgotten—that is genuinely fun to watch, and you're glad you discovered it. Such is the case with *Behind Green Lights*. I am willing to bet that you had never heard of this film. Badly dated and cheaply made, it was nonetheless the kind of movie that WWII audiences escaped to every weekend to watch at local movie houses in double features and talk about the next day. Films like this helped Americans escape grim headlines and deeply uncertain times. And as the old saying goes, they just don't write 'em like this anymore. Unlike much of the profanity- and graphic violence-laced dreck that passes for entertainment today, this sixty-four-minute film is actually enjoyable.

Not to be confused with the 1972 Marilyn Chambers surrealistic porno film *Behind the Green Door*—which I will *not* be reviewing for this book, sorry—the title of *Behind Green Lights* refers to the two round green lights displayed at the entrance of many big-city police stations around the time this movie was made. As the title says, the story involves the goings-on *behind* the lights (i.e., in the station house). In particular, the goings-on that occur in the course of a long night in a station in an "unnamed" city—can you say *New York?*

This film, like *Chicago Syndicate* (1955; see my review), had some actual production values and might in fact have been a trendsetter; it may have the paved the way for the too-many-to-list future films and TV cop shows (e.g., *Adam-12, Hill Street Blues*, etc.) about happenings in police stations during a defined period of time. That said, the film is definitely a curio, made at a time when police stations apparently had press rooms, fly-by-night doctors instead of the brilliant and always available MEs you see in most police dramas now, flower sellers, and no armories.

Allow me to explain: Police Lt. Sam Carson's—played by William Gargan, a prolific film, TV, and radio actor who voiced the title character in the wonderful *Barrie Craig, Confidential Investigator* radio show (1951–1956)—night shift at the station begins when a car with no driver comes to a stop on the station steps (i.e., *in front* of the green lights). Inside is the body of Walter Bard, a private investigator who specializes in getting the goods on people and then blackmailing them. Bard has been "shot through the pump"—as my favorite fictional detective, Archie Goodwin, would say—and a search of his body reveals a notebook that shows an appointment earlier that evening with someone named Janet Bradley.

This is one of those old detective movies where the detectives seem to know everything about everyone; Carson knows that Janet (Carole Landis, the star of One Million BC [1940] and known as the "Ping Girl" and "the Chest"—you get the idea) is the daughter of some famous guy who is running in some important election in a few days for some high-level office.

Carson brings Janet in for questioning and quickly learns that yes, (a) Bard had the goods on her father and was threatening to ruin the election unless she paid him off, (b) she pulled his gun on him, (c) she got the goods away from Bard, and (d) there were no witnesses, but no—so she says—(e) she didn't kill him. Carson has to think it over, so he puts Bradley in a side office, where she basically sits for much of the film.

But his office does not stay empty—it is beset by a crooked newspaper owner who also wants Janet's dad to lose the election and wants Carson to arrest the daughter and make it front-page news for the endless string of colorful reporters who are also running around looking for a scoop. Seems the reporters have an office right down the hallway. In fact, there seem to be many more members of the press than the police force in this station.

Unbeknown to Carson, his efforts to prove Bradley's innocence are thwarted at every turn by the unscrupulous physician on night duty, Dr. Yager. I knew a Dr. Yeager who was one of my mentors and a very good physician. Dr. Yager with no E, on the other hand, is no Quincy MD; he is embroiled in some kind of malpractice case, withholds medical information from Lt. Carson, and helps the crooked newspaper owner by spying on Carson and trying to get rid of Bard's body before it can be examined by a real ME. Alas, Jack Klugman is not scheduled to arrive until morning.

Soon, a flower lady, an embittered wife and her lawyer-lover, a comic-relief boxer, and more reporters are going in and out of Carson's office before—two flashbacks later—the truth about Bard's death is revealed. If you have read this far, then you are still with me, despite the fact that I have so far spoiled the endings of 42 movies for you. As a thank-you, I will not spoil this one for you; I think you should actually invest an hour of your life clock and watch this film. If you do, you'll see a young John Ireland appearing in just his second of nearly 120 movies as Lt. Carson's second-in-command and voice of reason.

However, the backstory of this movie is, alas, anything but fun. It was the last film for director Otto Brower, who died of a heart attack one month before *Behind Green Lights* was released by 20th Century Fox; technically, his uncredited work on the infamous *Duel in the Sun* (released larter in 1946) was the last directing he did. Apparently, while Brower knew all about the dangers of syphilis—he codirected the health-warning film *Sex Hygiene* with John Ford for the US military in 1942; see my review of *Dark Mountain*—he did not know about the cardiac dangers of his chain smoking. That did not come out until Surgeon General Luther Terry's 1964 report on smoking and cancer; see my review of *Armored Car Robbery*.

Carole Landis died just two years after this film from an overdose of Seconal she took after learning that Rex Harrison had no plans to leave his wife at the time, Lili Palmer, for her. Harrison, by the way, did not behave like the gallant Lt. Carson; he waited two hours before calling the police after finding Landis's body, had his lawyers destroy the suicide note she left him, and downplayed the relationship as "just a friendship," even though they were living together.

As with most bombs, watching *Behind Green Lights* will not change your life, but it's more fun to watch than, say, *Girl Gang* (1954); see my review—or then again, don't.

44

Dark Mountain (1944): A Certain Bogart Movie, Warmed Up and Served Scrambled

Don't get me wrong; I have great respect for many screenwriters. Some are remarkably talented. The BBC series *Unforgotten* is incredibly well written by someone named Chris Lang. But the sheer volume of material that screenwriters need to churn out at deadlines leads to what my wife and I often marvel at: a general lack of imagination. This accounts for the endless remakes, sequels, and other signs of phoning in a screenplay that are so prevalent in Hollywood.

Worse yet is what I call the *cluster phenomenon*, where screenwriters all get on a theme and focus on it because it seems to be profitable. Examples: 1992 was the year of the Christopher Columbus movies, including the not-bad *Christopher Columbus, the Discovery* and the genuinely terrible *1492: Conquest of Discovery*. The latter film is so awful that I do not recommend you see it even for its bombness unless you want to see a young Benecio Del Toro crucified and disemboweled by Indigenous Americans. In addition, 1998 was the year of the giant-meteor-hits-Earth movies, including *Armageddon* and *Deep Impact*. While the former was actually not bad, these films were just a recycling of the 1951 classic *When Worlds Collide*.

Similarly, the early 1940s were the years of the gangster-hides-up-in-the-mountains-and-gets-killed movies. The genre began with the iconic Bogart film *High Sierra* (1941). Made by Warner's, as all the great Bogart movies were—he was under contract at the time—the film has a plot that any movie geek can recite from heart, so here it goes: Bogart plays Roy "Mad Dog" Earl, a gangster who is really a good guy and wants to go straight but gets sucked into one more heist at a resort in the Sierras. Along the way to the predictably bad outcome, Roy helps a physically challenged girl, befriends a dog, and falls in love with Ida Lupino's character, whom he desperately wants to marry. But, alas, Roy is a tragic hero in the true Greek sense (look it up), and things do not end well for him—a spoiler alert for a film I'm not even reviewing: Roy hides out on a mountain where, thanks to the dog, he is lured out and killed by forest rangers.

Downbeat but popular, *High Sierra* was, of course, noticed by a writer and then a screenwriter for another studio (Paramount), who simply took the story and scrambled it into an omelet with even the title ripped off: *Dark Mountain* (1944). The good guy is now one of the forest rangers, who is dating the Ida Lupino character. After he gets a promotion, the forest ranger goes to his girlfriend's house to propose to her but—gasp—finds that she is married to the Bogart character. The movie can only have one hero, so the Bogart character is *not* a good guy. He kills a lot of people in an effort to run his stolen-goods operation, including his own flunky, played by Elisha Cook Jr. *Dark Mountain* is a genuine bomb complete with a low budget, generous use of stock footage, and a running time of fifty-six minutes. The makers could obviously not afford Bogart, but Cook must have come a lot cheaper and *reminded* audiences of Bogart because of his great supporting role as Wilber in *The Maltese Falcon* (1941).

Anyway, like *High Sierra*, *Dark Mountain* has the gangster character holing up in the mountains and—spoiler alert, but who cares?—dying a violent death that is again caused by a dog who is brave and loyal to the Ida Lupino character. The twist here is that the gangster shacks up with the Ida Lupino character, whom the forest ranger has hidden in a cabin to *protect her from the gangster*. The forest ranger visits her every day to bring her food and keep her company because, after all—shucks—he loves her and wanted to marry her. The gangster is clever; every time the forest ranger comes to the cabin for a visit, he hides in the back room until the ranger leaves. No wonder he's a criminal mastermind.

The forest ranger, by the way, has got to be one of the dumbest characters in movie history. He notices that the Ida Lupino character is eating an awful lot—this is 1944, so he can't ask her if she is pregnant—and leaving a lot of cigarette ashes around, especially for a nonsmoker. Still, he does not figure out that the gangster is there until the end of the movie. Yet it's a possible point of academic film discussion as to who is dumber, him or the gangster, who makes a getaway in a truck full of dynamite, hence the violent demise—more spoiler alert, but, really, who cares? That said, I promise I will not recommend that we break into study groups to discuss this point.

Given that it's a bomb, *Dark Mountain* stars no one you ever heard of except Cook. The gangster is played by the ubiquitous Regis Toomey—you've seen him on TV hundreds of times; the Ida Lupino character is played by Ellen Drew, who actually has a star on the Hollywood Walk of Fame, but who doesn't?; and the forest ranger is played by Robert Lowery. Lowery is best remembered for his role in the US military training film *Sex Hygiene* (1942; see my previous review of *Behind Green Lights*), in which he costarred with a pre-*Superman* George Reeves, warning GIs being shipped off to WWII about venereal disease. It sounds silly by today's standards, but penicillin was just being invented, and the film probably saved thousands of GIs from getting the clap. And, oh yeah, it was directed by John Ford.

Again, I have respect for screenwriters, but their all-too-frequent recycling of ideas is a disappointment. There are probably more films in the gangster-hides-up-in-the-mountains-and-gets-killed genre, but I frankly do not have the energy to look for them. Let me know if you find any more. Regardless, all such films likely have the same moral: if you want to be a gangster, avoid mountain hideouts and dogs.

45

Madmen of Mandoras (1963, 1968):
Also Known As . . .

I recently had the opportunity of meeting Donald C. Rogers. *The* Donald C. Rogers. Wait! You never heard of Donald C. Rogers?

Donald "Don" Rogers was a camera and boom operator who lived and worked in Hollywood until his retirement in 1996. Rogers was known at all the major studios as an available and reliable sound and camera person. As a result, he worked with all the great directors on ninety-two major films, including *South Pacific* (1959), *Nashville* (1975), *Rocky* (1976), *The Rose* (1979), *Ordinary People* (1980), *Ragtime* (1981), *My Favorite Year* (1982), *The Big Chill* and *The Right Stuff* (1983), *The Goonies* (1985)—during which he probably became familiar with the Northwest—*Ferris Bueller's Day Off* (1986), *Big* (1988), *Field of Dreams* and *Steel Magnolias* (1989), *The Shawshank Redemption* (1994), and *Mulholland Falls* (1996), just to name a few. And the ninety-two films listed in his filmography are just the ones he can remember; almost all of his work was uncredited because it was before the current times when everyone who even walks by a film set gets a credit, and the credits last a half an hour. I don't think Rogers cared about the credits; he was truly "in the business," worked with thousands of actors, and filmed an untold number of iconic scenes as part of his daily job. At his retirement, Rogers was recognized for his work with an honorary Oscar.

One of those iconic scenes is a shot that every reader of this book has likely seen: at the beginning of *The Sound of Music* (1965), there is an aerial sequence closing in on Maria von Trapp twirling on top of the Alps, which then cuts to her singing the title song. According to Rogers, he was hired by director Robert Wise to film it. Rogers rented a one-person helicopter, strapped the camera to the side, and in a twenty-minute period when the light was just right, he flew nine takes, knocking Julie Andrews down four times. If you look closely at the scene, you can see the grass around Andrews blow in the wind of the helicopter blades. Rogers fondly recalls that years later, he saw Andrews at a crowded party, and although there were a lot of celebrities there, she stood up when she saw him, stuck her finger in his chest, and shouted, "You! You're the one who knocked me on my arse!"

With such a filmography, I had to wonder: did Rogers ever film a bomb? I perused his work, and the answer, of course, is yes. After all, with all those movies under his belt, it's just math that he had. And what a bomb it was—none other than *Madmen of Mandoras* (1963). Wait! You never heard of *Madmen of Mandoras*?

Well, you probably have, but under a different title— more about that later. *Madmen* was made in 1963 by Crown International Pictures, which also released *The Skydivers* (see my review) the same year. Clocking in at seventy-three minutes, *Madmen* concerns a Mr. and Mrs. North-like couple named the Days, who mix drinks, make clever remarks, and exude the kind of sexuality allowed in 1960s B pictures. When a scientist friend is kidnapped and taken to the fictional South American country of Mandoras, they follow him down there, egged on by various foreign-looking people who keep popping up and warning them *not* to go and then getting killed. Seems the scientist has developed an antidote to something called G-gas, which, we are told, is odorless, tasteless, colorless, and kills everything in sight. When a movie like this is about something like that, the opportunities for bad jokes are endless, but I will restrain myself. Amazingly, the film was passed over by *MST3000*, even though it has a Rotten Tomatoes rating of *zero*, something I didn't even know was possible.

Anyway, no sooner do the Days arrive in Mandoras than they meet more mysterious characters and eventually learn through some dopey flashbacks that a bunch of Nazis have gathered in Mandoras to take over the world with G-gas and are forcing their scientist friend to reveal the formula for the antidote so that only the Nazis will have it. On the surface, the Nazi thing is just another terrible B-film gimmick, but as I have noted before, the people who funded these films in the '50s and '60s were mostly ex-GIs who had a real PTSD-based fear that the Nazis would come back—see my review of *The Yesterday Machine*—and knew that many were hiding in South America. Such films predated *The Boys from Brazil* (1978) by fifteen or more years.

Don Rogers tried his best with the sound—it isn't bad—and there is actually some good noir photography, but the low budget and short running time sink the movie. A "conference" of scientists consists of four people in a small room sitting in front of a wooden desk, and the army of Nazis has about seven soldiers. The dialogue is pretty silly, and as a result of extensive editing, the film makes no sense; characters appear and disappear, and at the end—spoiler alert—when the Days and their compatriots attack the Nazis, their gang of brave patriots includes a bunch of people you never saw before. A lot of movies are crowned the "worst movie of all time," but *Madmen* works hard for it.

Madmen had a limited run and would likely have been forgotten but for the power of TV. In 1968, late-late movie shows were all the rage on television—see the Preface and my reviews of *Fiend Without a Face* and *The Brute Man*—because they were used to sell products to insomniacs (this was before HSN or infomercials), and stations were hungry for bombs to show between the live ad spots. Crown put together a package of shelved films to sell to TV and wanted to include *Madmen*, but, ironically, it was too short for stations to buy. By that time, it was probably too late to find any of the film that was left on the cutting-room floor during the merciless editing process and, hence, maybe allow the film to make more sense. So, they hired UCLA film students—no, I don't think one of them was Tom Graeff (see my review of *Teenagers from Outer Space*)—to film an additional eighteen minutes to bring the running time to ninety-one minutes.

The students' footage, which opens the movie, tacks on more spy stuff that does nothing for the movie except make it even less coherent. Also, if you grew up in the '60s, you know that clothes, cars, and hairstyles changed dramatically from '63 to '68, so that despite the students' clever efforts to use similar cars, have actors hunched over so we can't see their faces, and film in the dark, their eighteen minutes are clearly a different movie and only make the film even more terrible. Worst of all, the students gave the movie a catchier, updated title, which guaranteed *Madmen* a place in "worst movie" history. Wait for it . . . *They Saved Hitler's Brain* (1968)!

So now that you know the origins of this infamous bomb, you may realize that at some point in your life, you either saw this thing or were smart enough to avoid it. I likely saw it on *Night Cap Theater*. More about that in Chapter 47. If you have not seen it, I will tell you that the famously exploitative title actually has something to do with the movie. Seems that in the flashbacks, the Days learn that Hitler did not die in that bunker but rather had his head removed by a crack team of surgeons who took it to Mandoras and kept it alive in a special glass contraption right out of *Donovan's Brain* (1953).

Hitler is played in the movie by an actor named Bill Freed, who plays the Fuhrer by sticking his head in a fish tank, shouting like Schicklgruber in a Three Stooges short, and making Hitler-like facial expressions. Freed's performance is the most frightening thing in the movie and made a big impression on me; it is what I most remember about the film after all the years since I first saw it.

By the way, a year before he "acted" in *Madmen*, Freed was in another film by another UCLA film student, a fellow named Francis Ford Coppola. Don't be impressed; Coppola got his start in movies making nudie films, and that movie, *Tonight for Sure* (1962), is pretty putrid and far too terrible to review even in this book. I only mention it because it also starred Marli Renfro, who was Janet Leigh's body double in Hitchcock's *Psycho*, so there is another link between one of the best movies in history and a couple of the worst. That said, there is no other reason to think about *Tonight for Sure*. Like G-gas, that film is tasteless, but unlike G-gas, it is not odorless. In fact, if only there had been some real G-gas around when *that* movie was made . . .

46

Devil on Wheels (1947):
The Venn Diagram Delivers Again

I turn again to the trusty Venn diagram to find the next bomb, this time intersecting Producers Releasing Corporation (PRC; see my review of *Murder Is My Business*), low-budget morality films (see my reviews of *The Flight That Disappeared* and *I Accuse My Parents*), and actors featured on Perry Mason (see my review of *Teenagers from Outer Space*) to find this little "training film" on the dangers of reckless driving, and a real forgotten gem, 1947's *Devil on Wheels*.

Let's take these elements of the diagram one at a time. First, the film was released by PRC, famous for B pictures that exploited sex and violence to churn out low-budget bombs that made a profit by appealing to the more puerile instincts of moviegoers. *Devil on Wheels* features bad driving that is so terrible it's funny. There are violent crashes, deaths, and all the female characters appear in a new fashion called the bikini. It was invented just one year before this film by French airplane engineer-turned-fashion designer Louis Reard, who named it after the Bikini

Atoll mushroom cloud, leading to a famous joke: "No bikini atoll!" No model would wear one at his fashion show, so Reard hired an exotic dancer. Yet PRC was quick to add these new bathing suits to the wardrobes on this film, thought to be the first movie to actually feature them.

Secondly, PRC staff knew what they were doing; theaters and audiences justified the viewing of these films because they purported to feature morals. In the case of this movie, the apparent lessons were "don't be a hypocrite" and "don't drive dangerously." But, as usual, the message was lost in ridiculousness; the character of the father in *Devil on Wheels* lectures everyone, including another driver who turns out to be a traffic judge, on driving while he drives at top speeds, weaving crazily in and out of traffic, blowing his horn, and causing accidents left and right. The scenes of his driving are laugh-out-loud funny and probably caused the audiences of the day to actually *disregard* the moral, asking themselves, *Who drives like that anyway?* Answer: all of the father character's family members follow his bad example except for his long-suffering wife, who—spoiler alert but so typical of these films—ends up a victim, which drives the point home (overdue bad pun). Also typical of these films, the moral is spoken out loud in courtroom scenes by a judge who looks right at the camera (see my review of *I Accuse My Parents*). Despite his car-crazed hot-rodding sons and their friends, the father is, of course, the *Devil on Wheels* in the title.

Thirdly, the central figure of the film, the father's youngest son, is played by Darryl Hickman, whom I was reminded about recently when I saw him on *Perry Mason*. Hickman was the brother of Dwayne Hickman, who played Dobie Gillis on TV, and there is an obvious resemblance. Hickman started out in Hollywood with a bang; his first role was in the wonderful

Ronald Coleman / Douglas Fairbanks Jr. / Madeleine Carroll / David Niven version of *The Prisoner of Zenda* (1937), and three years later, he was one of the Joad children in *The Grapes of Wrath*, which is widely considered one of the best films of all time; it was nominated for seven Academy Awards and won two.

Other roles in great films followed, but as he went through puberty, Hickman, like other child actors, found offers increasingly scarce. But you have to pay the bills—hence his work with PRC. Like a lot of players in bomb movies, Hickman later found roles on TV, including being cast as an extra on *Perry Mason*. That TV show was a veritable sink for bomb actors; Bryan Pearson (*Teenagers from Outer Space*) appears in "The Case of the Unwelcome Bride" episode (1961), and Hickman appears in "The Case of the Sleepwalker's Niece" (1957). Pearson's character was the murdered, and Hickman's was the murderer—double spoiler alert, high five! But unlike Pearson, Hickman found continued success on the small screen and went on to become a TV executive and acting coach. Interestingly, after a seventeen-year hiatus from the big screen, Hickman returned to act in *Network* (1976).

By the way, Hickman's girlfriend in the film was played by Terry Moore, who, like Hickman, was mostly in B films and TV but found her way into a few good movies. She was nominated for an Academy Award for *Come Back, Little Sheba* (1952), which starred Burt Lancaster and Shirley Booth, who won an Academy Award for her work in that film.

I'm not recommending *Devil on Wheels* unless you really enjoy watching such dated corn, like I do. The movie is surprisingly long for a bomb (ninety-nine minutes), which may tax your attention span, especially nowadays, but those crazy hot-rodding kids have wonderful dialogue ("It's a dilly!"; "I think it's the whammies!"), and their "bad" deeds make them look like Mother Teresa compared to teens in the current news. But the film is worth seeing for those driving scenes, especially if you need a few motorist tips before moving to Miami.

The Brute Man (1946): Stu Martin, Rondo Hatton, and Other Misunderstood Characters

I have alluded several times to a late-late bomb fest my dad, brothers, and I watched in the early '70s and loved: *Night Cap Theater*. Aired on various channels throughout the Northwest, its host, Stu Martin, showed bombs as a foil for frequent long breaks to hock various products. Using this technique, Martin could make a sixty-minute bomb last hours. The program usually started around 11 p.m., after the evening news, and ended around 1 or 2 a.m. In Portland, we watched Stu on channel 6, the local CBS affiliate KOIN.

There was nothing that Martin, a small, skinny, oily-looking guy with a dyed black fringe of hair, loud sports jackets, and a stereotypical salesman's manner, wouldn't sell or promote. Local restaurants were a favorite. Martin would carry his microphone into the place, interview the customers, and ask them what they were eating. No matter what they said, his reply was always the same: "Ooh, my favorite!" Martin had no shame and no ego; he sold toupees by putting them on his bald head one at a time and showing them off to the audience. Martin developed a bevy of loyal watchers, including my brothers and me, whom he called his "Night Cappers."

Martin's favorite sponsor was Seattle's Edgewater Inn, a hotel for which he developed the "Night Capper's Special Breakfast." The Edgewater, a hotel built out over Seattle's Elliot Bay for the 1962 World's Fair, was initially a hugely successful curio. When the Beatles came to Seattle in 1964, no hotel in the then-staid and conservative town—how times have changed—would give them a room except the Edgewater, resulting in the iconic photo of the band fishing from their room balcony. As the years passed, however, the Edgewater struggled because of its awkward location on Alaskan Way and competition from large chains. The proprietors hired Martin to talk them up, and he in turn invited his Night Cappers to go there and ask for a free continental breakfast that he had arranged for us: "a special roll, a cup of juice, and all the coffee you can drink!" All you had to do to get this, Stu told us, was drive the four hours to Seattle, find your way to the Edgewater, walk into the restaurant, and tell them, "I'm a Night Capper!" My brother Tom and I wanted to do it, but we didn't have a car and couldn't drive.

Stu is long gone, and his antics would be misunderstood by today's audiences, but the Edgewater remains, as do my memories of the many bombs I saw for the first time on Stu's program. It was on Stu's show that I first saw *The Brute Man* (1946), a film featuring another misunderstood guy, Rondo Hatton. Made by Universal at the tail end of the studio's horror craze (*Frankenstein*, *The Wolf Man*, *The Mummy*, etc.), and starring Hatton as a crazed killer known as the Creeper, *The Brute Man* was made just as Universal decided to get out of the B-film horror racket. So they sold it to—who else?—Producers Releasing Corporation (PRC).

Hatton was cast as the Creeper because he was genuinely frightening to audiences. Tall with a large, deformed face and large hands and feet, Hatton was every inch the 1940s audience's image of a mad killer. What the audiences didn't know, or didn't care about at the time, was that Hatton suffered from acromegaly, a disease that was poorly understood at the time and generally went unchecked until it led to the afflicted person's early death, usually from complications of heart disease or sleep apnea, which are present in 70 percent of cases. In 1946, the disease was not understood and went untreated; Hatton died of acromegalic heart disease at age fifty-two, just before *The Brute Man* was released.

Hollywood has always exploited acromegalics by casting them as scary or evil people, including Ted Cassidy (Lurch in *The Addams Family* TV show [1964–1966]) and Richard Kiel (Jaws in the James Bond movies). But by the late '70s and early '80s, the advent of serum assays and CAT scanning led to an understanding that 95 percent of cases of acromegaly are due to an excess of growth hormone secreted in adults by a benign tumor in the pituitary gland, leading to a post-puberty spurt in height and bone growth, especially in the hands and face. These discoveries led to effective treatments, including drugs to block growth hormone (bromocriptine, octreotide, and others), surgical removal of the tumors by neurosurgery, and focused radiation to the pituitary. While Cassidy died at forty-seven during an operation for his acromegaly-associated heart disease, modern acromegalics such as inspirational speaker Tony Robbins enjoy normal life spans due to treatment before serious complications occur, although they are left with the early sign of greatly increased height.

But in 1946, audiences didn't know or care about any of that, and neither did I in 1970, eight years before I started medical school and twelve years before the first CAT scanners. All we knew was that Rondo Hatton was scary-looking in *The Brute Man*, and it made perfect sense for him to be a crazed killer on the screen, seeking revenge on the people who deformed him in the "terrible accident" recounted in the film—which could be the only explanation we could see for his appearance—and loved only by a blind girl who could not see his face. The film also starred Tom Neal (see my review of *Detour*) and Donald McBride, an actor who bore a striking resemblance to J. Edgar Hoover and usually, not coincidentally, played law enforcement characters (see my review of *Michael Shayne, Private Detective*). Incidentally, McBride starred along Bogart in *High Sierra* (see my review of *Dark Mountain*).

As the years passed, and with my training as a physician, I came to understand the struggles of people like Stu Martin and Rondo Hatton. Too bad this was not the case for the creators of *MST3000*; in 1996, they mercilessly lampooned Hatton in *The Brute Man*. This led to the show getting a public black eye from many fans who objected to being invited to laugh at someone who suffered from a serious disfiguring disease that killed him shortly after the film was made.

It has been many years since that (probably) rainy night in Portland when I witnessed Stu Martin showing *The Brute Man*, and about a thousand interspersed live ads, on *Night Cap Theater*. In that time, I had forgotten most of the movie—sorry, Rondo—but I still remember Stu's antics like it was yesterday. Today, TV ads are mind-numbingly stupid, unnecessarily PC, and often downright insulting to our intelligence, and we do our best to avoid them, including getting special software to skip them and paying extra for stations that don't have them. The opposite was true with Stu; I think Night Cappers actually tuned in for his pitches because, like the bombs he showed, they were unintentionally funny and strangely endearing. Stu could be more entertaining than the actual films on his show.

48

Ring of Terror (1962): Abra Cadaver!
Another Bomb about Medical School

In my experience, there are two subjects that Hollywood just can't make a good movie about. The first is a movie about my hometown, Portland, Oregon. With the notable exception of *Mr. Holland's Opus* (1995), films set in the Rose City are usually terrible. To those who want to argue this point, I have three words for you: *Body of Evidence* (1993). Come to think of it, movies set anywhere in Oregon are usually bad, with the possible exceptions of *Stand by Me* (1986) and *The Goonies* (1985). And we can argue about *The Goonies*.

The second subject is medical school. As I said in the Preface, my two interests are medicine and old movies. That said, I have gone to medical school, seen a lot of films, and have yet to see a movie, old or new, that captured what medical school is really like. In fact, after I graduated from medical school, Hollywood cranked out a lot of bad films on this subject that made me feel like my experiences in school were woefully inadequate. All I did there was take stuff like anatomy, biochemistry, and physiology and then rotate through my clinical clerkships. I never fibrillated my classmates to the brink of death (*Flatliners* [1990]), brought the dead back to life with a serum I had invented (*Reanimator* [1987]), or cured childhood cancer by dressing up as a clown (*Patch Adams* [1998]).

While I was in medical school, I looked to old movies for inspiration but found none. From *Interns Can't Take Money* (1937)—a title that explains my paycheck from the hospital I was at—to *Not as a Stranger* (1955), bombs about medical school just depressed and confused me. Case in point, *Not as a Stranger* contains a scene where Dr. Robert Mitchum is talking to a female patient in the hospital and notices a small mole on her face. Later, Dr. Mitchum is talking to Dr. Frank Sinatra, who casually mentions that he removed the mole from the woman but did not send it to Pathology. Dr. Mitchum explodes in anger, telling him it was a melanoma—yikes. That causes Dr. Sinatra to get mad at Dr. Mitchum, and they stop speaking to one another. As a medical student who was interested in melanoma, and now as a surgeon who sees and treats a lot of it, I found that scene rather distressing; how did Dr. Mitchum know it was melanoma without a biopsy, and if he was right, was the woman going to get treatment? Later, Drs. Mitchum and Sinatra make up and agree not to mention the incident anymore. I found that *even more* distressing and spent the rest of the running time of *Not as a Stranger* worrying there was a woman running around out there with an untreated melanoma.

So, I was not surprised recently when I came across yet another stinker about medical school called *Ring of Terror*. Let me say at the onset that the story is set in the weirdest medical school ever. All the students are male, which was not unusual back in the day, but the guys are surrounded by a group of women who follow them around, join them at barbecues, and have beauty competitions. What these women are otherwise doing at the school is never clear. The students and the girls dance and hang out in the cafeteria and library, but most of the action occurs outdoors. Doesn't this school have any classrooms? And there is no anatomy lab; the students attend an autopsy—everyone in the movie pronounces it *ah-TOP-see*—which seems to be their only exposure to anatomy. Not surprisingly, most of the students get sick and faint.

All except one: Lewis Moffit, who, we are told, is twenty-one years old, although he is played by an actor who was forty-two at the time and looks every bit of it. Come to think of it, even by current standards, these are the oldest medical students I have ever seen. The plot involves the new students, like Lewis, trying to get into a medical fraternity and being assigned various hazing tasks. Because of his reputation for bravery, Lewis is assigned the task of stealing a ring—hence, the title—off the body of the *ah-TOP-see* subject. The ending, a real letdown, turns out to be—spoiler alert—just a variation on the old knife-through-the-poncho-in-the-graveyard routine.

Even though the film is only sixty-two minutes long, it still feels padded and boring. The movie features endless fat people jokes, typical of the time, and terrible dialogue; the *ah-TOP-see* scene involves a professor rattling off the names of various anatomic structures as he supposedly encounters them during the dissection, but in reality, he is naming structures that are not related anatomically to each other at all. The lines spoken between Lewis and his girlfriend and Lewis and his classmates are unintentionally hilarious. In contrast, there are a lot of intentional jokes that just aren't funny; the film can't decide whether it's a comedy or horror film, when in actuality it's just dumb. For a bomb fan like myself, what's not to like?

Fortunately, I saw *Ring of Terror* after I had already gone to medical school. If I'd seen it before, I might have been turned off to medical school and gone into a different field altogether, one that this film suggests is better, and safer, than medicine—like barbecue chef or beauty contest judge.

49

The House on Haunted Hill (1959): Did Alfred Hitchcock Rip Off William Castle?

If you use the Venn diagram to intersect Vincent Price (see my review of *Shock*), Elisha Cook Jr. (see my review of *Dark Mountain*), the favorite bomb subject of haunted houses (see my review of *Hillbillys in a Haunted House*), and the work of bombmeister William Castle (see my review of *The Fat Man*), you get exactly one film: 1959's *The House on Haunted Hill*, one of the most terrible and enjoyable bombs of all time.

The film opens with Vincent Price telling the audience that he has rented a "hundred-year-old haunted house" to hold a "party" to which he has invited five strangers: a psychiatrist, a typist, an airplane test pilot, a newspaper columnist, and a believer in the paranormal, who personally knew people who were murdered in the house. Price is a millionaire who will pay each attendee $10,000 to come to the party but only if they stay in the house until the next morning.

The house used for exterior shots in this film, by the way, was not one hundred years old. It was none other than the Ennis

House, an LA landmark built by Frank Lloyd Wright and modeled after a Mayan temple. Built in 1924, it was thirty-five years old when this movie was made; it *will* be one hundred years old next year. The Ennis House has been featured in dozens of films, usually for its unusual exterior. Director Castle filmed the interior shots on sets decorated with all the usual haunted house paraphernalia: cobwebs, old paintings, gas lamps, creaking floors, hidden passageways, and so on.

Anyway, it seems that Price's character and his beautiful fourth wife, played by Carol Ohmart, hate each other, and the "party" has something to do with that. I will not actually spoil the ending for you—after forty-seven spoiler alerts and a double spoiler alert—except to say that the ending is clever and the dialogue, especially the acrid exchanges between Price and Ohmart, is actually not bad. I will spoil the last line: Cook looks at the camera and tells the audiences that the ghosts will be coming for them next, directly ripping off the previously mentioned ending of *Invasion of the Body Snatchers* (1956). There was nothing Castle wouldn't "borrow" for his films.

Unlike Hitchcock, who achieved suspense and horror in unique and subtle ways, there was nothing subtle about Castle, and all his unsubtle attempts to scare audiences are here: storms, screams, ghosts, organs that play themselves, scary soundtrack, et cetera, et cetera. Castle also used gimmicks to convince audiences that his films were scary: electric buzzers strapped to seats, 3D glasses to "see" ghosts, nurses in the theater lobbies there to treat audience members who fainted, and in the case of this movie, plastic skeletons that "flew" over the audience's heads during the show, a gimmick Castle called Emergo.

Castle's attempts to scare audiences, lovingly recreated by John Goodman as a Castle-like moviemaker in *Matinee* (1993), were so desperate and routine that it seems impossible to believe that Hitchcock, who knew Castle was imitating him, had any admiration for the man. However, rumor has it that Hitchcock saw *The House on Haunted Hill*; liked the haunted house, black-and-white photography, and low budget; and came up with the idea for *Psycho* (1960). Rumor further has it that Castle returned the compliment by ripping off *Psycho* with his terrible *Homicidal* (1962).

Don't get me wrong; *The House on Haunted Hill* is still pretty bad, and it contains some serious goofs. Price shakes a bottle of champagne to make it explode, but when he opens it, there is not even a pop or any fizz. He fixes a drink below screen, complete with seltzer, ice, and so forth, but when he holds up the glass, it contains only water. One sad notation: The typist is played by an actress named Carolyn Craig, who died by self-inflicted gunshot wound eleven years after this film was made. At one point in the movie, she is handed a gun and told that if she has to, she should use it.

To compare Castle and Hitchcock, I suggest the following experiment: watch *Psycho* and *The House on Haunted Hill* on the same day. I think you'll reach this conclusion: *Psycho* is a masterpiece, but *The House on Haunted Hill* is fun.

50

Highway Dragnet (1954):
A U-Turn, No Pun Intended

And so I use the Venn diagram one more time to intersect not two but six predictors of bombness—Roger Corman (*The Last Woman on Earth, It Conquered the World*), the Salton Sea (*The Monster That Challenged the World*), Richard Conte (*The Blue Gardenia, Whirlpool*), Monogram Pictures / Allied Artists (*The Thirteenth Guest, King of the Zombies, The House on Haunted Hill*), Mary Beth Hughes (*I Accuse My Parents*), and Reed Hadley (*He Walked by Night*)—to come up with one more bomb: *Highway Dragnet*. As a kind of recap of this book, let's take these one at a time.

First, this was the film that Roger Corman got his start on as a co-screenwriter *and* an associate producer. Despite being credited for both, he felt unrecognized and that his future was not as a lackey for the big studios; more about that later. So, he went off on his own to produce films, using the money he earned here to make his first movie later that same year, 1954's *Monster from the Ocean Floor*.

Next, the Salton Sea. This landlocked, shrinking, foul-smelling saltwater lake in Southern California has recently been called the biggest environmental disaster in California history. But in the 1950s, it was a tourist destination for natives to stay at nice resorts, party, and birdwatch. Corman vacationed there, was interested by the flooded houses on its shoreline, and imagined a movie with a climactic chase through one of them. Accordingly, his original title for his resultant screenplay was *The House in the Sea*.

Richard Conte's appearance in *Highway Dragnet*, as I've said many times, was just math. A good Italian Catholic boy, Conte appeared in one hundred films, most of them bombs, so why not this one, which was made by none other than Allied Artists, the reincarnation of Monogram Pictures, the Poverty Row studio that knew how to grind 'em out and keep costs down.

Like so many Monogram/Allied films, and bombs in general, *Highway Dragnet* is filmed in black and white, is short (seventy-one minutes), and was shot in just ten days with a lot of budget corner-cutting. A key character in the film is mentioned, "heard from" later in a note, but never seen, thus saving the producers an actor's salary. A detective orders a "chopper" on the phone, then later gets a call telling him what the chopper saw, saving a helicopter rental. There's even a scene where someone is stuck in quicksand, only to be told that she will be fine because there is concrete below her feet, thus saving the prop department from buying a rope. And that's the irony; the "big studio" Corman wanted to get away from was Monogram/Allied!

Maybe he was angry that the studio changed the name of his screenplay to *Highway Dragnet*. Apparently, they wanted to cash in on the popularity of *Dragnet*, the radio (1949–1957) and TV (1951–1959) series developed by Jack Webb after he was inspired to create it by his work on *He Walked by Night* (1948).

Astute readers of this tome will note that *Night* was the first film I reviewed here, so we have come full circle—or maybe, since we are talking about a dragnet, it is more correct to say it's a U-turn.

And what a screenplay—it's really one long chase accompanied by the usual bomb elements of sex and violence. Jim Henry (Conte), a Korean War veteran with PTSD back when they still called it *battle fatigue*, is in Vegas on his way back home to the Salton Sea, when he encounters a blond floozy in a bar. Her name is Terry Reed, and she is played by none other than Mary Beth Hughes, who had a long B-picture career and played Kitty in *I Accuse My Parents* (see my review). One moment they are making flirtatious talk, then fighting, then kissing, and then the scene fades. That's the kind of movie it is. The next day, Jim is hitchhiking when he is arrested by a detective named Joe White Eagle—seems Terry was strangled with some kind of strap. Jim escapes Joe's custody, and the chase is on. Now called "the strap killer" by the press, Jim escapes the police by joining up with two women on their way to shoot a fashion spread at a resort. One of them is a model, changes into a bathing suit, and stays in it for the rest of the movie. They see Jim's picture in the paper and become his hostages, fleeing with him across the desert.

All the while, Jim proclaims his innocence, and he and the model slowly fall for each other. I will not actually spoil the ending; why bother? You can see it coming from a mile away. Along the way, another character gets shot, and it's that "just shot in the shoulder" routine so common to bombs that I have already debunked from a medical standpoint (see my review of *The Second Woman*). That character—OK, minor spoiler alert— is the person who directly links *He Walked by Night* to this film: Reed Hadley. Hadley, a veteran of over one hundred B pictures, plays Joe White Eagle in *Highway Dragnet* and is the narrator in *Night*. His deep, authoritative voice was also used to narrate several US Department of Defense films, including *The Nazi Plan* (1945), which was used as evidence at the Nuremberg trials.

The years have passed, and the Salton Sea has become a real stinker. It would be unfair to say the same about *Highway Dragnet*; even by today's over-the-top standards, it is fast-paced and keeps your attention. It was directed by one of the best art directors of the time, Nathan Juran, who was nominated for a Best Art Direction Oscar twice—for *How Green Was My Valley* (1942), for which he won, and *The Razor's Edge* (1946). "Awarded" the honor of directing B-grade sci-fi later in life, Juran nonetheless directed two great Ray Harryhausen films: *Twenty Million Miles to Earth* (1957) and *The 7th Voyage of Sinbad* (1958). In 1958, he also directed the cult film—there's that term again—*Attack of the 50-Foot Woman*, starring none other than Allison Hayes (see my review of *Chicago Syndicate*). So, if nothing else, *Highway Dragnet* ties together a lot of bombness and is therefore a great bomb to finish this book with.

Sitting at the bar at the beginning of the film, Terry shows Jim a picture of herself when she was modeling. He is impressed and tells her that she was "really beautiful then." It is a stupid remark, and she slaps his face, but it sums up how I feel about bombs. Often unattractive by modern standards, and largely forgotten now, they were really beautiful then.

Afterword

So many bombs, so little time. This selection of fifty bombs is but a sliver of the massive bomb arsenal available to the bomb fan. The reasons there are so many often short, forgotten, and not great films out there are, I think, threefold.

First, many bombs were made before the advent of television, and films like these were often the only way people could see entertainment on film. In fact, twelve of the films presented herein were made before the appearance of TVs in homes in the late '40s, and many were made shortly after that, when many Americans still did not have access to TV. I remember well when TV was still a novelty, and I especially remember when one of the neighbors on our block got a *color* television set; all of us kids in the neighborhood flocked to their house to lie on their living room carpet and watch the amazing sight of the NBC color peacock.

Second, the makers of these films were just trying to make a living, earn a little coin. To do this, they often had to resort to low-budget tricks and appeal to regional investors, promising them fame by putting their names on the big screen. Some, like Monogram Studios and Roger Corman's Filmgroup, found the right formula and had a lot of success. Others, like Ed Wood and Tom Graeff, simply never found the skill, resources, or luck they needed.

Third, the people who made these films were trying to *say something*—to tell a story they thought was worth telling, make a moral point, or comment on the times. I lovingly call these films *bombs*, but they are the blogs, snapchats, tweets, and podcasts of the twentieth century, and someday very soon, those twenty-first-century social media events listed above that were edgy and new will also become dated and forgotten. Yet whether old bombs or newer media events, all are attempts to reach out to others, all had something to say, and as such, they should be interesting in some way to any observer of history.

And so, as I stated in the Preface, I actually encourage younger readers—and I define that as anyone born after 1968, when the most recent bombs I review, *They Saved Hitler's Brain* and *The Green Slime,* were made—to not dismiss these so easily dismissed little films. Often silly, cheaply made, dated, or irrelevant by today's standards, they can still teach much about where we have been in the past and, maybe, where we should be going. They were not vegan, non-GMO, or cage-free—and certainly not smoke-free—but many were organically made, locally sourced, and handcrafted.

So, happy bomb-hunting! There is a treasure trove of old, largely forgotten, and often cheaply made films out there that can teach and entertain you indefinitely.

References

What, are you kidding? This is a book about obscure movies, and there is, by definition, not a lot written about them. The "facts" cited here came from the author's extensive knowledge of such films, whatever he could find on the internet, and, yes, Wikipedia.

Besides, after writing over 188 scientific papers and hundreds of national surgery test questions to date—note the shameless academic self-promotion (CV available on request)—which involved the citing of approximately 6,000 references, the author is getting tired of citing references. Also, none of those 6,000 references had anything to do with bomb movies. Trust me. But for those of you who really want a reference list, here is one, listed in order of appearance in the book. My apologies to the authors.

Hamilton, A. J. *The Scalpel and the Soul: Encounters with Surgery, the Supernatural, and the Healing Power of Hope*. New York: TartcherPerigee/Penguin Books, 2008.

Maltin, L. *Leonard Maltin's Movie Guide*. New York: Plume, 2015.

Chandler, Raymond. *Trouble Is My Business*. New York: Penguin/ Hammondsworth, 1950.

Hammett, Dashiell. *Nightmare Town*. West Valley City, UT: The Editorium, 2000.

https://radiospirits.com. Accessed October 23, 2021.

Kael, Pauline. *5001 Nights at the Movies: A Guide from A to Z.* New York: Holt, Rinehart, and Winston, 1982.

Ebert, Roger. *I Hated, Hated, Hated This Movie.* Kansas City: Andrews McMeel Publishing, 2000.

Ebert, Roger. *Your Movie Sucks.* Kansas City: Andrews McMeel Publishing, 2007.

Ebert, Roger. *A Horrible Experience of Unbearable Length.* Kansas City: Andrews McMeel Publishing, 2012.

Downs, M. "Two Leagues under the Sea." Palm Springs Life. https://www.palmspringslife.com/2-leagues-under-the-sea/. Accessed July 2, 2022.

Index

INDEX

215
Huntsman suits, 178, 180
Husky, Ferlin, 73–75, 77
Huston, Walter, 39
hypnotism, 29–30, 163–164

I

I Accuse My Parents (1944),
  107–109, 195, 196, 213,
  215
*I Am a Fugitive from a Chain
  Gang* (1932), 34
I Love Lucy (TV series, 1951–
  1957), 64, 84, 115
independent film, 37, 128, 157
India, 63–66
INH 7
Interns Can't Take Money
  (1937), 206
Invasion of the Body Snatchers
  (1956), 4, 28, 210
Ireland, John, 184
It Conquered the World (1956),
  153–155, 169, 213
It's a Wonderful Life (1946), 22

J

Jackie Gleason Show (TV series,
  1966–1970), 14
Jackson, Michael, 49
Jaekel, Richard, 149
Jail Bait (1954), 13, 47–53,
  81, 138
James, Sonny, 77
James Bond, 92, 201
Jazz Singer, The (1927), 21
Jeff Regan, Investigator (radio

series 1948), 2
Jenkins, Linda, 38
Jergens, Adele, 147
Joe Palooka, 27
Johnson, Tor, 134
John XXIII, Pope, 127
Jones, Chuck, 65
Jones, Lee, 2
Jones-Moreland, Betsy, 70–71
Jory, Victor, 64, 158
Julius Caesar against the Pirates
  (1962), 13–16
Juran, Nathan, 216

K

Kael, Pauline, 16, 161–162,
  164, 165
Karloff, Boris, 23, 64–65
Kelly, Emmett, 144
Kelly, Grace, 57, 177
Kelly, Jack, 166
Kennedy, John F., 111, 127
Kern, James V., 115–116, 117
Keys of the Kingdom (1944), 17
Kidnapped (1948), 33–34
Kiel, Richard, 75, 201
Kilburn, Terry, 128
Killing, The (1956), 57,
  103–104, 144, 145
King, Stephen, 43
King and I, The (1956), 170
King of the Zombies (1941),
  27–31, 213
Kipling, Rudyard, 63
kleptomania, 163–164
Kolb, Charles, 84
Korean War, 15, 134–135, 215

About the Author

Much to his surprise, John Vetto was born in Cincinnati, Ohio, a situation he corrected by moving his family to then-beautiful Portland, Oregon. This was a rather remarkable feat, as the author was only three years old at the time. When he is not viewing old, largely forgotten movies, the author pays the bills by working as a cancer surgeon. As you can tell, this is his first book.

For comments and accolades, John can be reached at:
jtvmd92@gmail.com

Made in United States
Troutdale, OR
05/05/2025